D0525149

Café & Restaurant Design

teNeues

Editor:	Martin Nicholas Kunz
Editorial coordination & Introduction:	Joachim Fischer
Translations:	SAW Communications, Mainz
Layout:	Thomas Hausberg
Imaging:	Jan Hausberg
Pre-press:	go4media. – Verlagsbüro, Stuttgart

Produced by fusion publishing GmbH Stuttgart / Los Angeles
www.fusion-publishing.com

Published by teNeues Publishing Group

teNeues Publishing Company
16 West 22nd Street, New York, NY 10010, USA
Tel.: 001-212-627-9090, Fax: 001-212-627-9511

teNeues Book Division
Kaistraße 18
40221 Düsseldorf, Germany
Tel.: 0049-(0)211-994597-0, Fax: 0049-(0)211-994597-40

teNeues Publishing UK Ltd.
P.O. Box 402
West Byfleet
KT14 7ZF, Great Britain
Tel.: 0044-1932-403509, Fax: 0044-1932-403514

teNeues France S.A.R.L.
4, rue de Valence
75005 Paris, France
Phone: 0033-1-55 76 62 05, Fax: 0033-1-55 76 64 19

www.teneues.com

ISBN:	3-8327-9017-9

© 2005 teNeues Verlag GmbH + Co. KG, Kempen

Printed in Italy

Bibliographic information published by Die Deutsche
Bibliothek. Die Deutsche Bibliothek lists this publication
in the Deutsche Nationalbibliografie; detailed bibliographic
data is available in the Internet at http://dnb.ddb.de

Contents

Americas

Asia / Pacific

Introduction

In the 21st century, eating out has as much to do with entertainment as with food. Restaurant owners, architects and designers nowadays create effective, themed and spectacular interiors, which are meant to seduce, impress and surprise us. It is a demanding job to create a room for guests to experience, when the design materials are a restaurant's space, gastronomy and economic basis. This task not only requires a successful concept, but also plenty of creativity and sensitivity. A central theme in this process is "spatial definition", or the design milieu, which includes the guest in a location and meets his expectations of a quality experience as well as his desires to feel personally involved. Sometimes, the framework for socializing, enjoyment and sensuality is created by totally simple rooms, which are almost everyday and familiar. Some-times, it is created by building up dreams that are translated into a room's architecture. The search for visions and contents is influenced by anticipating the highest possible attraction level. Turning dreams into reality is often the work of star designers, who design the most exciting

restaurants; they test architecture's fascination as adventure and the seductive power of vibrant urbanity. Venues become the designer's showroom and the public's stage.

A survey of up-to-date concepts and a study of the entire field reveals a tendency to set new quality standards. Despite globalization and stylistic unity—the striking thing is the different design initiatives of the examples shown here. They of course include color illustrations and are ordered by architects, from Andrée Putman, the Grande Dame of interior architecture, to the Enfant terrible, Philippe Starck, as well as Asian perspectives by Suppose Design Office.

Joachim Fischer

Einleitung

Im 21. Jahrhundert hat zum Essen ausgehen ebenso viel mit Unterhaltung wie mit Ernährung zu tun. Restaurantbetreiber, Architekten und Designer kreieren heute effektvolle, themenbezogene und spektakuläre Interieurs, die uns verführen, beeindrucken und überraschen sollen. Aus räumlichen, gastronomischen und wirtschaftlichen Faktoren eines Restaurants mit gestalterischen Mitteln einen Erlebnisraum zu schaffen, ist eine anspruchsvolle Aufgabe. Sie verlangt nicht nur ein gelungenes Konzept, sondern auch viel Kreativität und Sensibilität. Zentrales Thema ist hierbei eine „Raumbestimmung", die Milieugestaltung, die den Gast in den Ort mit einbezieht und seinen Erwartungen nach Erlebnisqualität und seinen Wünschen nach einem persönlichen Identitätsgefühl entspricht. Mal sind es ganz schlichte Räume, fast alltäglich und vertraut, manchmal aber auch gebaute Träume, in eine Raumarchitektur übersetzt, die den Rahmen für Geselligkeit, Genuss und Sinnlichkeit bildet. Die Suche nach Visionen und Inhalten ist geprägt von der Erwartung größtmöglicher Attraktivität. Die Umsetzung der Visionen in die Realität

erfolgt häufig durch Stardesigner, die die aufregendsten Restaurants entwerfen; die Faszination der Architektur als Abenteuer, die Anziehungskraft vitaler Urbanität wird erprobt. Lokalitäten werden zum Showroom der Designer, zur Bühne des Publikums.

Eine Bestandsaufnahme aktueller Konzepte und eine Auseinandersetzung mit dem gesamten Umfeld zeigt die Tendenz, neue Qualitätsmaßstäbe zu setzen. Trotz Globalisierung und einer stilistischen Vereinheitlichung – auffallend sind die unterschiedlichen Gestaltungsansätze der vorliegenden Beispiele. Diese sind durchweg farbig bebildert und nach Architekten gegliedert, von Andrée Putman, der Grande Dame der Innenarchitektur, über das Enfant terrible Philippe Starck bis hin zur asiatischen Sichtweise von Suppose Design Office.

Joachim Fischer

Introduction

Au 21ième siècle, sortir pour aller manger autant a voir avec le divertissement que la nourriture. Les restaurateurs, architectes et designers créent aujourd'hui des intérieurs remarquables, spectaculaires qu'ils déclinent sur différents thèmes et qui nous séduisent, nous impressionnent et nous surprennent. Concevoir l'aménagement d'un restaurant, en tenant compte des facteurs environnementaux, gastronomiques et économiques, pour en faire un espace attractif est un exercice ambitieux. Cela requiert non seulement un concept réussi mais aussi de la créativité et de la sensibilité. Le point principal est alors une « définition de l'espace », la création d'une ambiance qui met en relation le convive avec le lieu et qui répond à ses attentes de qualité et à ses désirs de trouver là la possibilité de s'identifier. Ce sont quelquefois des espaces sobres, presque habituels et familiers, parfois aussi la transposition de rêves réalisés en architecture d'intérieur, qui forme ainsi un cadre pour la convivialité, le plaisir et la sensualité. La recherche de visions et de volumes est déterminée par l'objectif de créer des lieux aussi séduisants

que possible. La transposition des visions en réalité est souvent réalisée par des designers célèbres qui conçoivent les restaurants les plus intéressants. C'est la fascination de l'architecture en tant qu'aventure, le pouvoir d'attraction d'une urbanité bien vivante qui est mise à l'épreuve. Des lieux sont transformés en salles d'expositions pour designers, en scène pour le public.

Un inventaire des concepts actuels et une confrontation avec l'ensemble de ce domaine révèlent qu'il y a une tendance à rechercher de nouveaux critères de qualité. Malgré la globalisation et une uniformisation des styles, la diversité des bases sur lesquelles s'appuie la conception des exemples dont on dispose ici est remarquable. Ceux-ci sont représentés en couleurs et ont été classés par architectes depuis Andrée Putman, la grande dame de l'architecture d'intérieur, en passant par Philippe Starck, l'enfant terrible, jusqu'aux points de vue asiatiques de Suppose Design Office.

Joachim Fischer

Introducción

En el siglo XXI el salir a comer tiene que ver tanto con la diversión como con la alimentación. Los dueños de restaurantes, los arquitectos y los diseñadores crean hoy interiores llenos de efecto, temáticos y espectaculares que nos han de seducir, impresionar y sorprender. Crear un espacio de vivencias a partir de los factores del espacio, gastronómicos y económicos de un restaurante con los medios del diseño es una tarea exigente. Reclama no sólo un plan bien conseguido sino también mucha creatividad y sensibilidad. El tema central en ello es una "determinación del espacio", la "configuración del medio" que toma en cuenta al cliente en el lugar y corresponde a sus expectativas de calidad de la vivencia y a sus deseos de un sentido personal de la identidad. A veces son espacios muy sencillos, casi cotidianos y familiares, pero a veces son también sueños construidos, traducidos a una arquitectura de interiores que forma el marco para la sociabilidad, los placeres y la sensualidad. La búsqueda de visiones y contenidos está caracterizada por la expectativa del mayor atractivo posible. La conversión de visiones en la

realidad ocurre a menudo por medio de diseñadores estrella que proyectan los restaurantes más excitantes; se ensayan la fascinación de la arquitectura como aventura, el poder de atracción de la urbanidad vital. Los espacios se convierten en el showroom de los diseñadores, en el escenario del público.

Un inventario de planes actuales y un análisis de todo el entorno muestra la tendencia de sentar bases de calidad. A pesar de la globalización y de una estandarización estilística –llaman la atención los diferentes planteamientos del diseño de los ejemplos presentados. Éstos están ilustrados en color en su totalidad y estructurados por arquitectos, desde Andrée Putman, la gran dama de la arquitectura de interiores pasando por el enfant terrible Philippe Starck hasta los puntos de vista asiáticos de los Suppose Design Office.

Joachim Fischer

Introduzione

Andare a cena al ristorante nel 21simo secolo è un evento culinario con valenza sociale oltre che nutrizionale. Oggi i gestori di locali, gli architetti e i designer creano interni spettacolari a tema e di grande effetto con l'intento di affascinarci, colpirci e sorprenderci. Voler trasformare, per fattori dettati da esigenze spaziali, gastronomiche o economiche, un ristorante in uno spazio tutto da vivere impiegando gli strumenti della creatività è un compito ambizioso. Esso richiede una progettazione spaziale riuscita oltre che tanta creatività e sensibilità. Il tema centrale è rappresentato da una "definizione spaziale", la creazione di un'atmosfera in grado di coinvolgere l'ospite, di soddisfare le sue aspettative di qualità e di personalità delle sensazioni che un locale deve essere in grado di trasmettere. A volte è la sobrietà la caratteristica principale che permette all'ospite di calarsi in un altro mondo, l'atmosfera quasi quotidiana e familiare; a volte si tratta di sogni concretizzati grazie agli espedienti dell'architettura d'interni, grazie ai quali si creano i presupposti ideali per la convivialità, il piacere, la sensualità. La ricerca di visioni e contenuti è

caratterizzata dalla voglia di visibilità. La traduzione delle visioni in realtà spetta spesso a designer d'eccezione, incaricati di progettare ambienti di grande effetto coreografico: e allora si mettono alla prova il fascino dell'architettura come avventura, la forza di attrazione esercitata dalla vitalità metropolitana. I locali diventano lo showroom dei designer, il palcoscenico del pubblico.

Il monitoraggio delle visioni più attuali e il confronto con il contesto più ampio mostrano un trend verso nuovi standard qualitativi. A dispetto della globalizzazione nella sua accezione più negativa e della tendenza all'uniformazione stilistica, ne emerge una policromia di approcci di cui vengono riportati alcuni esempi, presentati tutti a colori e secondo l'ordine degli architetti: partendo dalla grande dame dell'architettura d'interni, Andrée Putman, fino ad arrivare all'enfant terrible Philippe Starck e alle visioni orientali del team Suppose Design Office.

Joachim Fischer

The city of Graz is reflected in the outer skin of the café, which is floating as an artificial island on the Mur. Inner and outer worlds flow into each other, steel, glass and light make the building seem weightless. The result is a technically demanding avant-garde architecture, which escapes any attempt to categorize it.

Das Café, in dessen Außenhaut sich die Stadt Graz widerspiegelt, schwimmt als künstliche Insel auf der Mur. Innen- und Außenwelt fließen ineinander, Stahl, Glas und Licht lassen das Gebäude schwerelos erscheinen. Das Ergebnis ist eine technisch anspruchsvolle Avantgarde-Architektur, die sich jeder Kategorisierung entzieht.

Le café, dans la coque duquel se reflète la ville, flotte comme une île artificielle sur la Mur. Les espaces intérieur et extérieur confluent, l'acier, le verre et la lumière donnent l'impression que le bâtiment est en état d'apesanteur. Le résultat est une architecture d'avant-garde d'une technique de haut niveau qui échappe à toute classification.

El café, en cuya parte exterior se refleja la ciudad de Graz, nada en el Mur como una isla artificial. El mundo interior y el exterior fluyen uno en el otro, el acero, el vidrio y la luz hacen que el edificio parezca ingrávido. El resultado es una arquitectura de vanguardia con altas pretensiones técnicas que se sustrae a cualquier categorización.

Questo caffè, la città di Graz riflessa sulle pareti esterne come una seconda pelle, galleggia sul fiume Mur con le sembianze di un'isola artificiale. Mondo esterno ed interiore si completano in un gioco di riflessi: l'acciaio, il vetro e la luce donano all'edificio una leggerezza come priva di gravità. Il risultato è un esempio ambizioso architettonico di matrice avanguardistica sfuggevole a qualsiasi categorizzazione.

Acconci Studio

20 Jay Street 215
Brooklyn, NY 11201
USA
www.acconci.com

Photos by Harry Schiffer, Vito Acconci, courtesy Aiola Island

Aiola Island

Mur River
8011 Graz
Austria
www.island.aiola.at

Schönbrunn Palace is internationally famous and one of Vienna's most important tourist attractions. This is why the architects had to perform a balancing act: on the one hand, the café had to preserve exclusivity and the style of the location; and on the other hand it also had to meet the demands of modern tourism.

Schloss Schönbrunn ist weltbekannt und eine der größten Sehenswürdigkeiten von Wien. Daher mussten die Architekten einen Spagat bewältigen: Einerseits sollte das Café die Exklusivität und den Stil des Ortes wahren, andererseits aber auch den Anforderungen des modernen Tourismus gerecht werden.

Le château de Schönbrunn est mondialement connu et une des attractions les plus importantes de Vienne. C'est pourquoi les architectes devaient réussir à concilier là deux choses : d'une part le café devait préserver l'exclusivité et le style du lieu, d'autre part cependant être à la mesure des exigences d'un tourisme moderne.

El Palacio de Schönbrunn es mundialmente conocido y una de las atracciones turísticas más importantes de Viena. Por ello, los arquitectos tuvieron que superar un dilema: Por un lado, el café debía conservar la exclusividad y el estilo del lugar pero, por otro lado, también debía corresponder a las exigencias del turismo moderno.

Il castello di Schönbrunn, noto in tutto il mondo, rappresenta una delle attrazioni più importanti della città di Vienna. Per gli architetti un vero dilemma: la necessità di conciliare l'esclusività e l'eleganza di un luogo con le esigenze del turismo moderno.

Architekturbüro Franziska Ullmann und Peter Ebner

Windmühlgasse 9/26
1060 Vienna
Austria

Photos by Margherita Spiluttini

Café Gloriette

Schloss Schönbrunn
1130 Vienna
Austria

The restaurant has large windows that incorporate the form of the neighboring market stalls when they are opened. The problem of lighting was solved in an original way by covering the ceiling with a synthetic sheet on which coffees beans are magnified to giant size and illuminated from behind.

Das Lokal ist mit großen Fensterflächen ausgestattet, die aufgeklappt die Form der umliegenden Marktstände einbeziehen. Die Frage der Beleuchtung wurde originell gelöst, indem man die Decke mit einer von hinten beleuchteten Kunststoffplane verkleidet hat, auf der stark vergrößerte Kaffeebohnen abgebildet sind.

Le lieu a été conçu avec de grandes baies vitrées qui, quand elles sont basculées, rappellent la forme des stands du marché avoisinant. La question de l'éclairage a été résolue de façon originale en doublant le plafond d'une bâche de plastique éclairée par derrière, sur laquelle sont représentés des grains de café très agrandis.

El local está equipado con grandes ventanales que, abiertos, incluyen la forma de los puestos del mercado de los alrededores. La cuestión de la iluminación fue solucionada de un modo original revistiendo el techo con una lona sintética alumbrada por detrás sobre la cual hay reproducidos granos de café muy ampliados.

Il locale è dotato di grandi finestre a tutta parete che, una volta aperte esternamente verso l'alto, si mimetizzano perfettamente con le bancarelle circostanti. Il problema dell'illuminazione è stato risolto con una soluzione originale, rivestendo il soffitto con un enorme telo di plastica illuminato da dietro sul quale sono raffigurati grandissimi chicchi di caffè.

Dietrich | Untertrifaller Architekten

Arlbergstraße 117
6900 Bregenz
Austria
www.dietrich.untertrifaller.com

Photos by Ignacio Martinez

Deli am Naschmarkt

Stand 421-436
1040 Vienna
Austria
www.naschmarkt-deli.at

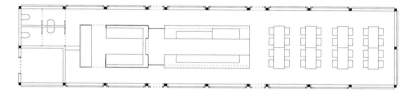

The modern interpretation of a French brasserie is located in the MoMu or Fashion Museum. The restaurant is overflowing with low-key luxury: travertine for the flooring, walls and bars, as well as tinted glass and black lacquer. The furnishing is of wood, steel and leather and specially made for the brasserie.

Die moderne Interpretation einer französischen Brasserie ist im MoMu, dem Modemuseum, beheimatet. Das Restaurant verströmt diskreten Luxus: Travertin für Böden, Wände und Tresen sowie getöntes Glas und schwarzer Lack. Die Möblierung aus Holz, Stahl und Leder wurde speziell für die Brasserie angefertigt.

La version moderne d'une brasserie française s'est établie dans le MoMu, le musée de la mode. Le restaurant exhale un luxe discret : du travertin sur les sols, murs et le bar ainsi que du verre teinté et de la laque noire. Le mobilier en bois, métal et cuir a été fabriqué spécialement pour la brasserie.

La interpretación moderna de una Brasserie francesa está establecida en el MoMu, el Museo de la Moda. El restaurante emana un lujo discreto: travertin para los suelos, las paredes y los mostradores así como vidrio matizado y barniz negro. El mobiliario de madera, acero y cuero fue elaborado especialmente para la Brasserie.

L'interpretazione moderna della brasserie francese si trova al MoMu, il museo d'arte. Il ristorante trasmette la sensazione di un lusso discreto: travertino per i pavimenti, le pareti ed il bancone nonché vetro colorato e lucidi elementi d'arredo laccati in nero. I mobili in legno, acciaio e pelle sono stati creati appositamente per la brasserie.

Vincent van Duysen Architects

Lombardenvest 34
2000 Antwerp
Belgium
www.vincentvanduysen.com

Photos by Alberto Piovano

Brasserie National

Nationalestraat 32
2000 Antwerp
Belgium
www.nationalantwerp.be

The restaurant on the first floor of a tennis club presents itself as a room within a room and the focus is mainly on round shapes. Dynamics and tension are key themes and they enrich the atmosphere. The room design is finished off by classic pieces of furniture that have an organic feel.

Als Raum im Raum präsentiert sich das Restaurant im ersten Stock eines Tennisklubs und konzentriert sich primär auf runde Formen. Thematisiert werden Dynamik und Spannung, von denen ein jede die Atmosphäre bereichert. Das Raumkonzept wird durch organisch anmutende Möbelklassiker abgerundet.

Le restaurant au premier étage d'un club de tennis se présente comme un espace dans un espace et opte en premier lieu pour des formes rondes. Les thèmes sont la dynamique et la tension et ils créent à eux deux une atmosphère. De beaux meubles classiques évoquant des formes organiques donnent la touche finale à la conception de cet espace.

Como una sala dentro de la sala, el restaurante se presenta en la primera planta de un club de tenis concentrándose en primer lugar en las formas redondas. Se tematizaron la dinámica y la tensión y ambas enriquecen la atmósfera. El plan para el espacio se complementa con clásicos del mueble que causan una impresión orgánica.

Puntando sull'intersecazione volumetrica degli spazi, questo ristorante (ubicato al primo piano di tennis club) colpisce soprattutto per la predominanza delle forme arrotondate. Dinamismo e tensione, elementi che arricchiscono l'atmosfera, ne sono i protagonisti tematici. Sottolineano l'idea di fondo complementi d'arredo classici dalle sembianze quasi organiche.

Atelier Kunc

Komunardů 43
Holešovice, Prague 7
170 00 Czech Republic
www.atelierkunc.com

Photos by Tomáš Rasl

Club Restaurant Stromovka

Za Císařským mlýnem 33
Prague 7
Czech Republic

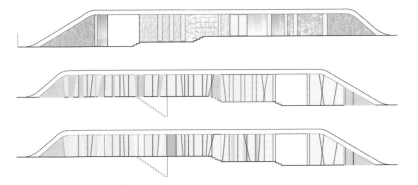

The *leitmotiv* is change. Variable, colorful and flowing styles of wall cladding made of fiber glass fill the rooms and at the same time integrate the seating arrangements. The music, menu, light and furnishing change on a daily basis in the popular cafeteria, in keeping with the overall design concept.

Das Leitmotiv lautet Veränderung. Variable, farbige und fließend anmutende Wandverkleidungen aus Fiberglas durchziehen die Räume und integrieren gleichzeitig die Sitzgelegenheiten. Getreu dem Gesamtkonzept ändern sich Musik, Menu, Licht und Einrichtung in der angesagten Cafeteria täglich.

Le leitmotiv est le changement. Des revêtements muraux modulables en fibres de verre, colorés, qui séduisent aisément traversent les espaces et intègrent en même temps les siéges. Fidèle au concept de base, la musique, le menu, la lumière et l'aménagement change, dans la cafétéria très tendance, tous les jours.

El leitmotiv consiste en el cambio. Los revestimientos de fibra de vidrio variables, de colores y que causan una impresión de fluidez recorren las salas e integran al mismo tiempo los asientos. Fiel al plan general, en la cafetería que hace furor cambian diariamente la música, el menú, la luz y la decoración.

Motivo conduttore è il mutamento: rivestimenti delle pareti colorati e polifunzionali in fibra di vetro creano un leitmotiv ricorrente in tutti gli ambienti con salottini integrati. In linea con la realizzazione architettonica sono anche la musica, il menù, la luce e l'arredamento che variano di giorno in giorno in questa caffetteria alla moda.

Johannes Torpe Studios

Skoubogade 1,1
1158 Copenhagen
Denmark
www.johannestorpe.com

Photos by Jens Stoltze

Supergeil

Nørrebrogade 184
2200 Copenhagen
Denmark

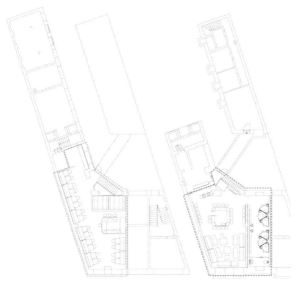

The Delhi Deli is a kind of box made of zinc and incorporated into the existing building. The planners equipped the design of this box with modern furnishings and defined by simple forms. Their influences were traditional patterns and colorful Indian kitsch.

Das Delhi Deli ist als eine Art Box aus Zink in das bestehende Gebäude geschoben worden. Die Gestaltung dieser Box wurde von den Planern, angeregt durch traditionelle Muster und farbenfrohen indischen Kitsch, modern und von schlichten Formen bestimmt ausgestattet.

Le Dehli Dehli est comme une sorte de cube en zinc glissé dans le bâtiment existant. Les concepteurs de ce cube, inspirés par les motifs traditionnels et le kitsch indien très coloré, l'ont aménagé d'une façon moderne caractérisée par de formes sobres.

El Delhi Deli fue encajado en el edificio existente como una especie de caja de zinc. Estimulados por diseños tradicionales y por el kitsch indio lleno de colorido, los proyectistas dotaron a esta caja de una configuración moderna y determinada por las formas sencillas.

Il Delhi Deli è stato integrato nell'edificio esistente come una sorta di scatola in zinco. Per la sua realizzazione gli arredatori si sono ispirati a motivi tradizionali e allo stile kitsch indiano dai colori vivaci, arricchito da un tocco di sobria modernità e da forme semplici.

Project Orange

1st Floor, Morelands, 7 Old Steet
London EC1V 9HL
UK
www.projectorange.com

Photos by Georgia Glynn-Smith

Delhi Deli

30 Battersea Rise
London SW11 1EE
UK
www.delhideli.com

The bar and restaurant of the Parisian luxury hotel captivate with their majestic decor and are a popular meeting point in the fashion world. Patrick Jouin added neutral materials to the exclusive rooms. They are shown off to full effect by light staging that changes from cool blue to warm orange.

Bar und Restaurant des Pariser Nobelhotels bestechen durch ihr prächtiges Dekor und sind ein beliebter Treffpunkt der Modewelt. Patrick Jouin fügte den exklusiven Räumen neutrale Materialien hinzu. Eine von kühlem Blau bis zu warmem Orange wechselnde Lichtinszenierung setzt die Räume eindrucksvoll in Szene.

Le bar et le restaurant du grand hôtel parisien séduisent par leur aménagement fastueux et sont un des lieux de rencontre les plus appréciés du monde de la mode. Patrick Jouin est intervenu dans les espaces raffinés avec des matériaux neutres. Une installation lumineuse qui varie du bleu froid à un orange chaud met les espaces remarquablement en scène.

El bar y el restaurante del lujoso hotel parisino impresionan por su fastuosa decoración y son un apreciado punto de encuentro del mundo de la moda. Patrick Jouin agregó materiales neutrales a las exclusivas habitaciones. Una escenificación de luces cambiante desde el azul frío hasta el naranja cálido pone en escena las habitaciones de forma impresionante.

Bar e ristorante dell'hotel parigino di gran lusso affascinano per la splendida scenografia e costituiscono un salotto popolare del mondo della moda. Patrick Jouin ha aggiunto agli ambienti esclusivi dei materiali neutrali. La gamma cromatica cangiante (dal freddo blu al caldo arancione) ottenuta con effetti luminosi dona agli ambienti un'atmosfera coreografica.

Patrick Jouin

8, Passage de la Bonne Graine
75001 Paris
France
www.patrickjouin.com

Photos courtesy Patrick Jouin PR

Plaza Athénée

25, Avenue Montaigne
75008 Paris
France
www.plaza-athenee-paris.com

Philippe Starck worked magic to create a fascinating, surreal empire of crystal out of the former palace of the Viscountess of Noailles. In this luxurious location, private flair, modernity and new "bourgeois chic" enter an exciting liaison.

Philippe Starck hat das einstige Palais der Vicomtesse de Noailles in ein faszinierendes surrealistisches Reich aus Kristall verzaubert. Ein luxuriöser Ort, an dem privates Flair, Moderne und neuer „Bourgeois-Chic" eine spannende Verbindung eingehen.

C'est avec un véritable enchantement que Philippe Stark a fait du seul palais de la Comtesse de Noailles un empire de cristal surréaliste et fascinant. Un lieu luxueux où se mêlent de manière intéressante la touche personnelle, le moderne et le nouveau style « bourgeois chic ».

Philippe Starck transformó el antiguo palacio de la vizcondesa de Noailles en un fascinante imperio surrealista de cristal. Un lugar lujoso en el que el encanto privado, lo moderno y el nuevo encanto burgués están unidos de forma fascinante.

Philippe Starck ha trasformato l'ex Palais della Vicomtesse de Noailles in un regno di cristallo al contempo surrealista e affascinante, conferendo al luogo lussuoso che esso già era un fascino più intimo, moderno, con un tocco di "Bourgeois-Chic", elementi che sposandosi danno vita ad una combinazione del tutto interessante.

Philippe Starck Network

18/20, Rue du Faubourg du Temple
75011 Paris
France
www.philippe-starck.com

Photos by Claude Weber

The Cristal Room Baccarat

11, Place des Etats-Unis
75116 Paris
France
www.baccarat.fr

With exposed stone walls and austere furnishing the architects succeeded in recreating the typical subversive character of "squatters' charm". Guests sit below gentle lighting on a rostrum on chic, white cushions and listen to lounge-style house music, while dining mostly on vegetarian food.

Mit seinen kahlen Steinwänden und einer kargen Möblierung gelang es den Architekten, den typisch subversiven „Hausbesetzer"-Charme erneut zu kreieren. Die Gäste sitzen unter mildem Licht auf einem Podest in schicken, weißen Polstern und vernehmen zu meist vegetarischen Speisen loungige House-Musik.

Les architectes ont réussi, avec les murs de pierre nus et le mobilier sobre, à recréer le charme subversif typique des squats. Les convives sont assis sur une estrade, dans d'élégants fauteuils blancs sous un lumière douce et peuvent entendre, en dégustant les plats le plus souvent végétariens, de la house musique.

Mediante las paredes de piedra peladas y un escaso mobiliario el arquitecto consiguió crear de nuevo el típico encanto subversivo de los "ocupas". Los clientes están sentados bajo una luz suave en elegantes asientos tapizados en blanco sobre un estrado y escuchan música house de lounge mientras comen, por lo general, comidas vegetarianas.

Optando per le fredde pareti in pietra ed uno scarso mobilio gli architetti sono riusciti a ricreare il fascino tipicamente sovversivo da "occupazione abusiva". Gli ospiti siedono su eleganti poltrone su una piattaforma elevata immersa in una luce tenue con sottofondo musicale da lounge gustando piatti per lo più vegetariani.

Soeren Roehrs, Assistenz: Laura Rave

Charlottenstraße 95
10969 Berlin
Germany
www.soerenroehrs.com

Photos by Dirk Wilhelmy

Cookies Cream

Charlottenstraße 44
10117 Berlin
Germany
www.cookiescream.com

The architects have created an integrated room structure out of two shops and a bar. The furniture is the unifying element. The material was selected so that it developed a "patina": stained wood, leather and brown-colored steel for the furniture, solid, waxed boards for the floor.

Aus zwei Läden und einer Bar haben die Architekten eine zusammenhängende Raumstruktur geschaffen. Vereinendes Element ist die Möblierung. Das Material wurde so ausgewählt, dass es „Patina" entwickelt: gebeiztes Holz, Leder und brunierter Stahl für die Möbel, massive geölte Dielen für den Boden.

Les architectes ont créé à partir de deux magasins et un bar une structure d'espace cohérente. Le mobilier tient lieu d'élément de liaison. Les matériaux qui ont été choisis vont se patiner avec le temps : du bois lasuré, du cuir et de l'acier bruni pour les meubles, des parquets en bois massif huilé pour le sol.

De dos tiendas y un bar los arquitectos crearon una estructura del espacio continua. El elemento vinculante es el mobiliario. El material fue elegido de modo que desarrollase pátina: madera barnizada, cuero y acero fosfatado para los muebles, tablas masivas lubrificadas para el suelo.

Partendo da due negozi e da un piano bar gli architetti hanno creato una struttura unica. Filo conduttore dell'arredamento è il mobilio. Il materiale è stato scelto così da ricreare l'effetto patina: legno verniciato, pelle ed acciaio brunito per i mobili, legno massiccio trattato con olio per i pavimenti.

Ascan Tesdorpf

Friedrichstraße 235
10969 Berlin
Germany
www.at-a.de

Photos by Ascan Tesdorpf

Engelbrecht

Schiffbauer Damm 6/7
10117 Berlin
Germany
www.engelbrecht-berlin.de

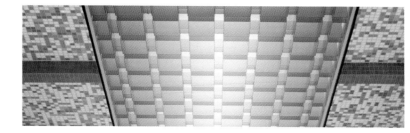

Due to the deep proportions of the room, the guest space is organized along the central table and flanked by a shelf that reaches to the ceiling. If required, the 5 m long table where guests stand can be lowered and extended sideways. Alternating use of color and material selection create interlocking zones and spatial peripheries that are unclearly defined.

Aufgrund der tiefen Raumproportion ist der Gastraum entlang des zentralen Tisches gegliedert und von einem deckenhohen Regal flankiert. Der 5m lange Stehtisch kann bei Bedarf zur Tafel abgesenkt und verbreitert werden. Wechselnde Farbigkeit und Materialwahl bilden ineinander verzahnte Bereiche und unscharfe Raumgrenzen.

En raison de la profondeur de la pièce, la salle à manger est organisée autour de la table centrale et est encadrée d'une étagère de la hauteur d'un plafond. La table haute de cinq mètres de long peut être au besoin élargie et abaissée en table à manger. Les coloris changeants et le choix des matériaux créent des espaces aux frontières floues qui s'emboîtent les uns dans les autres.

Debido a la profunda proporción del espacio, el comedor está estructurado a lo largo de la mesa central y flanqueado por una estantería de la altura del techo. La mesa para estar de pie, de 5 m de longitud, puede bajarse y ensancharse cuando es necesario. Una coloración variable y la elección de materiales crean recintos ensamblados uno en el otro y demarcaciones del espacio difusas.

Per le esigenze di profondità l'area ricettiva è suddivisa in lunghezza grazie al tavolo centrale e alla scaffalatura a tutta parete che lo affianca. Il tavolo elevato, lungo 5 m, può essere ampliato ed abbassato così da poter fungere da tavola con posti a sedere. La policromia cangiante e la scelta dei materiali creano degli spazi poco delimitati che intersecandosi confluiscono l'uno nell'altro.

unit-berlin

Leipziger Straße 55
10117 Berlin
Germany
www.unit-berlin.de

Photos by Noshe

Tressette

Kurfürstendamm 36
10719 Berlin
Germany

The architecture of the modern and successful restaurant is by Meinhard von Gerkan, the corporate design by Peter Schmidt and the artworks by Oliver Jordan. The combination of glass and steel, slate and pear wood, walls with *stucco lustro* and Thonet lever chairs is optically imposing.

Die Architektur des modernen und erfolgreichen Restaurants stammt von Meinhard von Gerkan, das Corporate Design von Peter Schmidt und die Kunstwerke von Oliver Jordan. Optisch prägend ist die Verbindung von Glas und Stahl, Schiefer und Birnbaumholz, Wänden mit *stucco lustro* und Thonet-Freischwingern.

L'architecture du restaurant moderne qui a beaucoup de succès est de Meinhard von Gerkan, le Corporate Design de Peter Schmidt et les œuvres d'art de Oliver Jordan. Le lieu est caractérisé par l'association du verre et du métal, de l'ardoise et du bois de poirier, des murs avec *stucco lustro* et avec des chaises Thonet avec leur base tout en courbes.

La arquitectura del moderno restaurante de éxito procede de Meinhard von Gerkan, el Corporate Design de Peter Schmidt y las obras de arte de Oliver Jordan. Está caracterizado visualmente por la unión de vidrio y acero, pizarra y madera de peral, las paredes con *stucco lustro* y las sillas "Thonet".

L'architettura di questo ristorante moderno e di successo è opera di Meinhard von Gerkan, il Corporate Design di Peter Schmidt e le opere d'arte di Oliver Jordan. Di grande effetto estetico è soprattutto la combinazione di vetro e acciaio, ardesia e legno di pero, pareti in *stucco lustro* e sedie Thonet.

gmp – Architekten von Gerkan, Marg und Partner

Elbchaussee 139
22763 Hamburg
Germany
www.gmp-architekten.de

Photos by Dirk Wilhelmy, Klaus Frahm

Jägerstraße 54
10117 Berlin
Germany
www.vau-berlin.de

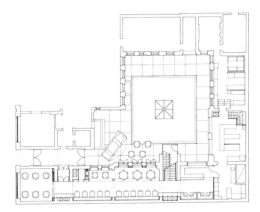

The name refers to a trendy quarter in Miami. The combination of bar, café, restaurant and event location is completed in gastronomic terms by New World Cuisine, which is popular in Miami. Light and colors are used to full effect, in order to separate or combine rooms with one another.

Der Name bezieht sich auf ein In-Viertel in Miami. Gastronomisch abgerundet wird die Mischung aus Bar, Café, Restaurant und Event-Location durch die in Miami gepflegte New World Cuisine. Licht und Farben werden auf wirkungsvolle Weise eingesetzt, um Räume abzugrenzen bzw. miteinander zu verbinden.

Le nom se réfère à un quartier à la mode de Miami. La cuisine New World soignée de Miami apporte la touche finale à ce lieu à la fois bar, café, restaurant et qui se loue aussi pour des évènements. La lumière et les couleurs sont utilisées de manière remarquable afin de séparer ou relier les espaces.

El nombre se refiere a un barrio de moda en Miami. En lo gastronómico la mezcla de bar, café, restaurante y event location se completa por la New World Cuisine que se cultiva en Miami. La luz y los colores fueron empleados con un gran efecto para delimitar las salas o bien unirlas unas con otras.

Il nome si riferisce ad un quartiere alla moda di Miami. L'interessante combinazione di bar, caffè, ristorante nonché location per eventi viene completata dall'offerta gastronomica all'insegna della tradizione, cara a Miami, della New World Cuisine. Luce e colori vengono impiegati con abilità per creare degli effetti che servono ora a delimitare gli spazi, ora a farli confluire l'uno nell'altro.

Bender Design

Hertelsbrunnenring 13
67657 Kaiserslautern
Germany
www.bender-design.de

Photos by Friedrich Busam

Coconut Groove

Kaiserstraße 53
60329 Frankfurt
Germany
www.coconut-groove.de

Different spatial worlds are presented in a former slaughter house. 3deluxe has designed them down to the last detail. The interdisciplinary concept, which is effectively put into action, links architectural, multi-media and graphic elements to form a symbiotic whole.

In einem ehemaligen Schlachthofgebäude präsentieren sich nun unterschiedliche Raumwelten, die 3deluxe bis ins kleinste Detail gestaltet hat. Das interdisziplinäre Konzept verbindet architektonische, multimediale und grafische Elemente zu einem symbiotischen Ganzen, effektvoll in Szene gesetzt.

Dans un ancien bâtiment d'abattoir, on trouve maintenant des espaces ambiants différents que 3deluxe a aménagés jusque dans les moindres détails. Le concept interdisciplinaire, mis en scène de façon remarquable, associe des éléments architectoniques, multimédiatiques et graphiques et forme ainsi un ensemble symbiotique.

En el edificio de un antiguo matadero se presentan ahora diferentes mundos de espacios que 3deluxe ha diseñado hasta en el más pequeño detalle. El plan interdisciplinario, puesto en escena con gran efecto, une en un conjunto simbiótico los elementos arquitectónicos, los de multimedia y los gráficos.

In un ex mattatoio trovano spazio diversi mondi percettivi che 3deluxe ha trasformato senza trascurare il minimo dettaglio. Il progetto di ristrutturazione a tutto tondo – realizzazione di grande effetto – unisce elementi architettonici, multimediali e grafici trasformandoli in un tutto armonioso.

3deluxe

Schwalbacher Straße 74
65183 Wiesbaden
Germany
www.3deluxe.de

Photos by Emanuel Raab

Cocoon Club

Carl-Benz-Straße 21
60386 Frankfurt
Germany
www.cocoonclub.net

The design concept is based on elements of water, earth, fire and air. The bar is coupled with the water element, the garden with the earth. The motif in the lounge is flickering movements of fire. The terrace is the place of endless space, here, the element of air dominates over all other elements.

Das Konzept basiert auf den Elementen Wasser, Erde, Feuer und Luft. Die Bar ist dem Element Wasser, der Garten der Erde zugeordnet. Die flackernden Bewegungen des Feuers sind das Motiv der Lounge. Die Terrasse ist Ort der unendlichen Weite, hier thront das Element Luft über allen anderen Elementen.

Le concept a pour base les éléments eau, terre, feu et air. Le bar est consacré à l'élément eau, le jardin à la terre. Les mouvements vacillants du feu sont le thème du hall. La terrasse est le lieu de l'espace infini, ici c'est l'élément air qui règne sur tous les autres.

El plan se basa en los elementos del agua, la tierra, el fuego y el aire. El bar está asignado al elemento del agua, el jardín al de la tierra. Los movimientos oscilantes del fuego son el motivo del lounge. La terraza es el lugar de la extensión interminable, aquí reina el elemento del aire sobre todos los otros elementos.

La concezione architettonica si rifà agli elementi naturali acqua, terra, fuoco e aria. Il bar simboleggia l'elemento dell'acqua, il giardino quello della terra. Motivo del lounge bar-salotto è il movimento tremolante della fiamma. La terrazza è il luogo della spazialità infinita, il luogo in cui l'elemento aria predomina su tutti gli altri.

de Picciotto und Wittorf Architekten

Bei den Mühren 91
20457 Hamburg
Germany

Photos by Klaus Frahm / artur

Die Welt ist schön

Neuer Pferdemarkt 4
20359 Hamburg
Germany
www.dieweltistschoen.net

In a former fish-packaging hall, a refuge for optical purists and connoisseurs was created in this restaurant. 120 seats, mostly at individual tables, are available in a white, hall-like room. A good third of this space is taken up by the open show kitchen with the sushi bar.

Mit dem Restaurant wurde in einer ehemaligen Fisch-Packhalle ein Refugium für optische Puristen und kulinarische Genießer geschaffen. 120 Plätze, zumeist an Einzeltischen, stehen in einem weißen, hallenartigen Raum zur Verfügung. Gut ein Drittel der Fläche nimmt die offene Showküche mit der Sushi-Bar ein.

Dans cette ancienne halle aux poissons, on a créé ce restaurant qui est un havre pour ceux qui aiment la pureté des lignes et pour les gourmets. Dans cet espace blanc, qui a gardé son caractère de halle, se trouvent 120 places, la plupart à des tables individuelles. La cuisine ouverte avec le bar à sushis occupe un bon tiers de la surface.

Con el restaurante se creó un refugio para puristas visuales y sibaritas culinarios en una antigua nave de empaquetamiento de pescado. 120 asientos, en su mayoría en mesas individuales, están a disposición en una sala blanca en forma de nave. Un buen tercio de la superficie la acoge la cocina –espectáculo abierta con el bar de sushi.

Con questo ristorante ubicato in un'ex sala confezionamento pesce è stato creato un rifugio per i puristi dell'estetica e per palati raffinati. 120 posti a sedere, per lo più in tavolini singoli, sono disposti in un ambiente bianco così ampio da sembrare un padiglione. Un buon terzo della superficie è coperto dalla cucina show cooking con sushi bar.

Udo Strack

Mühlenkamp 4
22303 Hamburg
Germany
www.udostrack.com

Photos by Henssler & Henssler

Henssler & Henssler

Große Elbstraße 160
22767 Hamburg
Germany
www.h2dine.de

A modern and stylish atmosphere greets guests behind the facade of the gymnasium, built in 1889. In the ten meter high and spacious room, new and rebuilt elements dominate: long, solid tables in the bar, partitions to the restaurant and lounge area and round-arched windows, opened to make doors.

Hinter der Fassade der 1889 erbauten Turnhalle erwartet die Gäste ein modernes und stilvolles Ambiente. In dem zehn Meter hohen und weitläufigen Raum dominieren Ein- und Umbauten: lange massive Tische in der Bar, Abtrennungen zum Restaurant- und Loungebereich und zu Türen durchbrochene Rundbogenfenster.

Une ambiance moderne et de bon goût attend les convives derrière la façade du gymnase construit en 1889. Dans le vaste espace de dix mètres de haut, ce sont les éléments intégrés et construits qui dominent : de longues tables massives dans le bar, les séparations de la salle de restaurant et du hall d'entrée et les fenêtres en arc de plein cintre qui ont été percées en porte.

Detrás de la fachada del gimnasio construido en 1889 espera a los clientes un ambiente moderno y lleno de estilo. En el amplio espacio de una altura de diez metros dominan los montajes y las reformas: mesas largas masivas en el bar, separaciones con el recinto del restaurante y del lounge y ventanas en arcos de medio punto partidas formando puertas.

Dietro la facciata di una palestra costruita nel 1889 si nasconde un locale dall'atmosfera moderna ed elegante. La sensazione di grande spazialità, favorita dalle pareti alte 10 m, è sottolineata dalle strutture costruite o ricavate dalla ristrutturazione: lunghi tavoli massicci nella zona bar, divisori nella zona ristorante e lounge, finestre con arco a tutto sesto trasformate in porte.

Frank B. Theuerkauf

Daimlerstraße 2
21357 Bardowick
Germany

Photos by Markus Bachmann

Turnhalle St. George

Lange Reihe 107
20099 Hamburg
Germany
www.turnhalle.com

Montag–Freitag
12⁰⁰–15⁰⁰

Sonntagsbrunch
11⁰⁰ 14⁰⁰ für € 14.50
inkl. Kaffee u. Tee

Mittags – karte

* Gemüsecreme-Suppe mit Croutons   3,90

* Gebackene Champignons mit Kräuterquark   5,90

* Mexikanischer Bohnensalat   6,90
  mit gebratenen Rinderfiletstreifen

* Asiapfanne, Rindfleisch in Sojasoße   7,90
  und Wokgemüse

* Fischvariation, gegrillt mit Flussenbis   8,90
  Röstkartoffeln und Salatbeilage

* Pasta mit frischen Pfifferlingen   7,90

* Pizza Capricciosa   6,90

* Rabarberendbeermousse   4,20

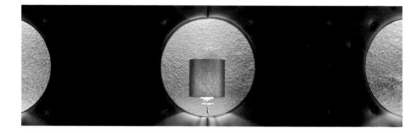

The ceiling and plaster-work were left untreated in the Comercial. The materials used in the redevelopment are a contrast to that: oak, steel, leather and a specially printed material as a wall covering. Atmospheric lighting can be altered to suit changing light conditions at day and night.

Im Comercial wurden die Decke und der Putz unverkleidet gelassen. Im Kontrast dazu stehen die beim Ausbau verwendeten Materialien: Eiche, Stahl, Leder und ein speziell bedruckter Stoff als Wandbespannung. Eine atmosphärische Beleuchtung passt sich den wechselnden Lichtverhältnissen bei Tag und Nacht an.

Au Comercial les plafonds et le crépi ont été laissés nus. Les matériaux utilisés pour la rénovation : le chêne, l'acier, le cuir et, comme tenture murale, un tissu spécialement imprimé viennent former un contraste. Un éclairage qui crée une atmosphère s'adapte à la luminosité changeante du jour et de la nuit.

En el Comercial se dejaron sin revestir los techos y el revoque. Con ello contrastan los materiales empleados en la ampliación: roble, acero, cuero y una tela estampada especialmente como revestimiento. Una iluminación atmosférica se adapta a las condiciones de luz variables durante la noche y el día.

Nel Comercial soffitto e intonaco sono stati volutamente lasciati allo stato grezzo. Ne nasce un contrasto naturale con i materiali impiegati per la ristrutturazione: quercia, acciaio, pelle ed una stoffa stampata appositamente che funge da rivestimento delle pareti. L'illuminazione atmosferica si adegua ai diversi giochi di luce e ombre durante il giorno e la notte.

Architekten Stadler + Partner

Balanstraße 9
81669 Munich
Germany
www.planungswelt.de

Photos by Andreas Pohlmann

Bar Comercial

Theatinerstraße 16
80333 Munich
Germany

Until now, the Lounge has been a unique project that was created from the transferal of a firm's corporate identity to gastronomy. The blue bubbles of mobile telephone network O2 are depicted in a glass wall and the rooms are designed, according to the company's guidelines, in a young, modern and cosmopolitan style.

Die Lounge ist ein bisher einmaliges Projekt, das aus der Übertragung der Corporate Identity eines Wirtschaftsunternehmens auf die Gastronomie entstand. Die blauen Wasserblasen des Netzbetreibers O2 sind in einer Glaswand verbildlicht, die Räume nach Unternehmens-Richtlinien jung, modern und kosmopolitisch gestaltet.

La Lounge est un projet jusqu'à maintenant unique qui a été créé en reportant l'image de marque de l'entreprise sur la restauration. Les bulles d'eau bleues de l'opérateur de réseau O2 sont illustrées dans un mur de verre, les espaces sont aménagés selon les directives de l'entreprise dans un esprit jeune, moderne et cosmopolite.

El Lounge es un proyecto único hasta ahora que surgió de la aplicación a la gastronomía de la Corporate Identity de una empresa de economía. Las burbujas de agua azules del operador de red O2 están ilustradas en una pared de vidrio, las habitaciones están configuradas de forma joven, moderna y cosmopolita según las directrices de la empresa.

Il Lounge rappresenta un progetto a tutt'oggi unico nato dalla trasposizione dell'idea di corporate identity aziendale dal settore prettamente industriale a quello gastronomico. Le bolle di acqua blu dell'operatore O2 sono riproposte su una parete di vetro, gli interni (secondo i dettami dell'azienda) sono arredati secondo criteri giovani, moderni e cosmopoliti.

Schmidhuber + Partner

Nederlingerstraße 21
80638 Munich
Germany
www.schmidhuber.de

Photos by Quirin Leppert

Lounge 2

Bayerstraße 3-5
80335 Munich
Germany

Charles Schumann rules here, the bright star in the sky of German cocktail bars, the author of popular cocktail recipe books and successful restaurateur. The architects have created an unfussy, Mediterranean atmosphere with high-quality materials in Schumann's new Bar am Hofgarten.

Hier regiert Charles Schumann, leuchtender Stern am deutschen Cocktail-Himmel, Autor beliebter Cocktail-Rezeptbücher und erfolgreicher Gastronom. Mit edlen Materialien haben die Architekten in Schumann's neuer Bar am Hofgarten eine schnörkellose und mediterrane Atmosphäre geschaffen.

C'est ici le domaine de Charles Schumann, brillante étoile dans le monde du cocktail en Allemagne, auteur de livres de recettes de cocktails et restaurateur renommé. Dans le nouveau Bar am Hofgarten de Charles Schumann, les architectes ont créé avec des matériaux de qualité une atmosphère méditerranéenne sans fioritures.

Aquí reina Charles Schumann, la estrella luminosa en el cielo alemán de los cócteles, autor de apreciados libros de recetas de cócteles y gastrónomo de éxito. Con materiales nobles los arquitectos crearon una atmósfera sin adornos y mediterránea en el nuevo Bar am Hofgarten de Schumann.

Regno incontrastato di Charles Schumann, astro brillante nel firmamento tedesco dei barmen nonché autore di popolari libri di ricette per cocktail e gastronomo di successo. Nel nuovo Schumann's Bar am Hofgarten gli architetti hanno saputo creare un'atmosfera sobria di ispirazione mediterranea grazie all'impiego di materiali nobili.

Boesel Benkert Hohberg Architekten

Horemansstraße 28
80636 Munich
Germany
www.boesel-benkert-hohberg.de

Photos by Boesel Benkert Hohberg Architekten

Schumann's Bar am Hofgarten

Odeonsplatz 6-7
80539 Munich
Germany
www.schumanns.de

The windows in the cafeteria are like shop windows. Built-in elements structure the long expanse of the room and define the front and back entrance. The materials and patterns define horizontal and vertical axes, which structure both room shapes, lights, wall shelving and furniture.

Die Verglasung der Cafeteria hat Schaufenstercharakter. Einbauten gliedern den lang gestreckten Raum und bestimmen Vorder- und Hintereingang. Materialien und Muster definieren horizontale und vertikale Achsen, welche die beiden Raumkörper, Leuchten, Wandregale und das Mobiliar strukturieren.

Les baies vitrées de la cafétéria ont un caractère de vitrine. Des meubles encastrés divisent la pièce étirée en longueur et déterminent les entrées avant et arrière. Les matériaux et motifs définissent les axes horizontaux et verticaux qui structurent les deux parties de l'espace, les luminaires, les étagères et le mobilier.

El acristalamiento de la cafetería posee carácter de escaparate. Los módulos dividen la sala que se extiende longitudinalmente y condicionan las entradas delantera y trasera. Los materiales y diseños definen ejes horizontales y verticales los cuales estructuran ambos cuerpos, las lámparas, las estanterías de las paredes y el mobiliario.

Le vetrate della caffetteria creano un effetto vetrina. Mobili ad incasso suddividono la lunga sala predisponendo entrata anteriore e posteriore. I materiali e i motivi decorativi scelti definiscono gli assi orizzontali e verticali che conferiscono struttura volumetrica agli elementi spaziali, alle lampade, alle mensole alle pareti e al mobilio.

Oda Pälmke

Choriner Straße 32
10435 Berlin
Germany
www.odapaelmke.de

Photos by Walter Niedermayr

Cafeteria der Freien Universität Bozen

Via Sernesi 1
39100 Bolzano
Italy
www.unibz.it

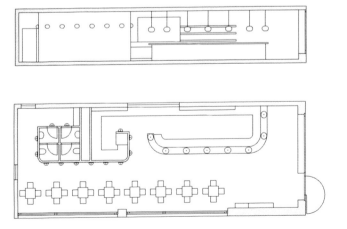

The elements of air, light, fire and water are defining characteristics of the Princi Bakery Café. Water flows from a newly laid fountain, an open fire in the bakery, which is on view, is a reminder that bread was originally baked in a wood-burning stove and large windows illuminate the room.

Die Elemente Luft, Licht, Feuer und Wasser bestimmen die Charakteristik des Princi Bakery Café. Wasser rinnt aus einem eingelassenen Brunnenstein, eine Feuerstätte in der einsehbaren Backstube erinnert daran, dass Brot ursprünglich im Holzofen gebacken wurde und große Fenster erhellen den Raum.

Ce sont les éléments air, lumière, feu et eau qui caractérisent le café Princi Bakery. De l'eau s'écoule d'une fontaine, un foyer dans le fournil à la vue de tous rappelle que le pain était à l'origine cuit dans des fours à bois et de grandes fenêtres amènent de la lumière dans la pièce.

Los elementos del aire, la luz, el fuego y el agua condicionan la característica del Princi Bakery Café. El agua mana de un manantial empotrado, un brasero en la panadería visible recuerda que el pan fue cocido originalmente en el horno de leña y unas grandes ventanas iluminan la sala.

Gli elementi predominanti del Princi Bakery Café sono aria, luce, fuoco ed acqua. L'acqua scorre copiosa da una fontana, il focolare del forno visibile da fuori ricorda che originariamente il pane veniva cotto nel forno a legna e grandi finestre rischiarano l'ambiente.

Claudio Silvestrin Architects

Unit 412 Kingswharf
301 Kingsland Road
London E8 4DS
UK
www.claudiosilvestrin.com

Photos courtesy Claudio Silvestrin Architects

Princi Bakery Café

Piazza Venticinque Aprile
20123 Milan
Italy
www.princi.it

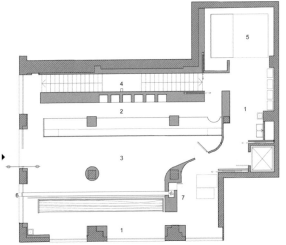

Pianta generale

1 laboratorio
2 banco vendita
3 zona consumazic

At first sight, the Sonora blu created by Studiomonti looks like a living room. The rooms of the restaurant and bar are dark and unfold an intensive effect. Wall cladding that looks like window blinds provides shelter from the outside world and softly falling light underlines the private atmosphere.

Auf den ersten Blick gleicht das von Studiomonti geschaffene Sonora blu einem Wohnzimmer. Die Räume des Restaurants mit Bar sind dunkel und entfalten eine intensive Wirkung. Jalousienähnliche Wandverkleidungen schirmen die Außenwelt ab und weich einfallendes Licht unterstreicht die private Atmosphäre.

À première vue le Sonora blu, agencé par Studiomonti ressemble à une salle de séjour. Les salles du restaurant et du bar sont sombres et produisent un effet intense. Le revêtement mural fait penser à des stores et protège du monde extérieur tandis que la lumière douce souligne l'atmosphère privée.

A primera vista el Sonora blu creado por Studiomonti parece el comedor de una vivienda. Las salas del restaurante con bar son oscuras y despliegan un efecto intenso. Los revestimientos similiares a persianas protegen del mundo exterior y una luz que entra suavemente resalta la atmósfera privada.

Di primo acchito il Sonora blu, creato da Studiomonti, assomiglia ad un salotto. Gli ambienti scuri del ristorante con salotto-bar trasmettono delle sensazioni intense. Dei rivestimenti alle pareti simili a veneziane fungono da schermo del mondo esterno, una luce soffusa sottolinea l'atmosfera di intimità.

Studiomonti s.r.l.

Piazza S. Erasmo, 1
20121 Milan
Italy
www.studiomonti.com

Photos by Alessandro Ciampi

Sonora blu

Viale Ravenna, 6
48016 Milan
Italy

Vincenzo Corvino and Giovanni Multari designed the existing restaurant consisting of two rooms—cafeteria and art gallery. The interior architecture is distinguished by purist lines and is marked by the deliberately simple materials of maple, beech, marble, steel and glass.

Vincenzo Corvino und Giovanni Multari gestalteten das aus zwei Räumen – Cafeteria und Kunstgalerie – bestehende Restaurant. Die Innenarchitektur zeichnet sich durch eine puristische Linienführung aus und wird geprägt durch die betont schlichten Materialien Ahorn, Buche, Marmor, Stahl und Glas.

Vincenzo Corvino et Giovanni Multari ont aménagé ce restaurant composé de deux espaces, une cafétéria et une galerie. L'architecture d'intérieur se distingue par des lignes puristes et se caractérise par l'accent mis sur la sobriété de matériaux comme l'érable, le hêtre, le marbre, l'acier et le verre.

Vincenzo Corvino y Giovanni Multari configuraron el restaurante que consta de dos salas: cafetería y galería de arte. La arquitectura interior se destaca por un trazado de líneas purista y se caracteriza por los materiales marcadamente sencillos: arce, haya, mármol, acero y vidrio.

Vincenzo Corvino e Giovanni Multari hanno trasformando l'architettura interna dell'esistente ristorante costituito da due ambiti, la caffetteria e la galleria d'arte, in un ambiente dalle linee puriste in cui spiccano materiali volutamente sobri quali acero, faggio, marmo, acciaio e vetro.

Corvino+Multari Architetti Associati

Via Ponti Rossi, 117
80131 Napoli
Italy
www.gruppoprogetti.it

Photos by IDRA Photo Riproduzioni

Il Ristorante del Consiglio

Centro Direzionale di Napoli - Isola F13
80143 Napoli
Italy

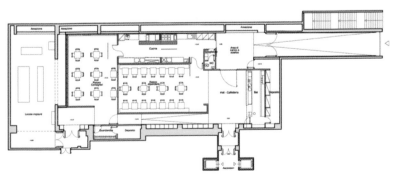

The sustained use of polished steel and marble, restrained use of color and generous use of photographic prints are a contrast here to the building, which is a 19th century palace. Two aspects of the Eternal City were combined with the new design: its traditional past and today's vitality.

Konsequenter Einsatz von poliertem Stahl und Marmor, gedeckte Farbgebung und großflächige Fotodrucke stehen hier im Kontrast zum Gebäude, einem Palais aus dem 19. Jahrhundert. Bei der Neugestaltung wurden zwei Aspekte der Ewigen Stadt vereint: ihre traditionelle Vergangenheit und die heutige Vitalität.

L'utilisation conséquente d'acier poli et de marbre, des teintes estompées et des tirages photo de grand format forment un contraste avec le bâtiment qui est un palais du 19ième siècle. Lors de la rénovation deux aspect de la Ville éternelle ont été conjugués : son passé traditionnel et la vitalité de son présent.

El empleo consecuente del acero pulido y del mármol, la coloración apagada y las amplias impresiones fotográficas están aquí en contraste con el edificio, un palacio del siglo XIX. En la remodelación se unieron dos aspectos de la Ciudad Eterna: su pasado tradicional y la vitalidad actual.

L'impiego coerente di acciaio lucidato e marmo, la scelta cromatica all'insegna della sobrietà e le immagini fotografiche a tutta parete creano un contrasto con l'edificio in cui è ubicato questo ristorante, un palazzo del 19simo secolo. La ristrutturazione ha saputo valorizzare due aspetti della città eterna: il suo passato ricco di tradizione e la sua vitalità contemporanea.

Tihany Design
Adam D. Tihany, Rafael Alvarez, Peter K. Lu, Andréa Riecken

135 West 27th Street
New York, NY 10001
USA
www.tihanydesign.com

Photos by Janos Grapow

La Frusta

Exedra
Piazza della Repubblica, 47
00185 Rome
Italy
www.boscolohotels.com

Supperclubs are more than restaurants: whoever dines here is introduced to the newest trends in eating, art, fashion, music, video, performance and style. And that all happens at once. The Supperclub that was opened in Rome is an attractive contrast to the historical building due to its glamorous interior.

Supperclubs sind mehr als Restaurants: Wer hier diniert, dem werden die neuesten Formeln für Essen, Kunst, Mode, Musik, Video, Performance und Style präsentiert. Und das alles auf einmal. Der in Rom eröffnete Supperclub steht mit seinem glamourösen Interieur in reizvollem Widerspruch zum historischen Gebäude.

Les Supperclubs sont plus que des restaurants : on présente ici aux convives les dernières nouveautés dans le domaine de la cuisine, de l'art, de la mode, de la musique, de la vidéo, de la performance et du style. Et tout ceci à la fois. L'intérieur glamour du Supperclub qui s'est ouvert à Rome, forme un contraste intéressant avec le bâtiment historique.

Los Supperclubs son más que restaurantes: A quien come aquí se le presentan las fórmulas más nuevas para comida, arte, moda, música, video, performance y style. Y todo ello a la vez. El Supperclub abierto en Roma, con su atractivo interior, contrasta de forma encantadora con el edificio histórico.

I Supperclub sono molto più che ristoranti: chi vi pasteggia assapora non solo le ultime proposte in fatto di gastronomia, ma anche di arte, moda, musica, video, performance e style. Tutte in un sol boccone. Con il suo interno tutto glamour, il Supperclub inaugurato a Roma crea un contrasto affascinante con l'edificio storico in cui è ubicato.

concrete architectural associates

Rozengracht 133 III
1016 LV Amsterdam
The Netherlands
www.concrete.archined.nl

Photos courtesy concrete architectural associates

Supperclub

Via de' Nari, 14
00186 Rome
Italy
www.supperclub.com

This seaside restaurant is influenced by minimalist design, which corresponds to the modern *Zeitgeist*. Guests sit either on classic furniture in an inner room dominated by stainless steel, glass and neon lighting, or they can enjoy the spectacular view of the sea from the terrace.

Minimalistisches Design prägt dieses direkt am Meer gelegene Restaurant, das dem modernen Zeitgeist entspricht. Die Gäste sitzen entweder auf Möbelklassikern in einem von Edelstahl, Glas und Neonlicht dominierten Innenraum oder können von der Terrasse aus den spektakulären Blick aufs Meer genießen.

Un design minimaliste, qui correspond à l'esprit du temps donne le ton dans ce restaurant situé tout au bord de la mer. Les hôtes peuvent s'asseoir sur des sièges classiques dans un espace intérieur, où l'acier, le verre et l'éclairage au néon dominent, ou profiter depuis la terrasse de la vue spectaculaire sur la mer.

El diseño minimalista caracteriza este restaurante situado directamente frente al mar que corresponde al espíritu moderno de la época. Los clientes se sientan en clásicos del mueble en una sala interior dominada por el acero fino, el vidrio y la luz de neón o pueden disfrutar de las espectaculares vistas al mar desde la terraza.

Il design minimalista è la caratteristica predominante di questo ristorante sul mare dalle linee architettoniche del tutto attuali. Gli ospiti possono scegliere di sedersi all'interno, su classici dell'arredamento calati in un'atmosfera in cui predominano acciaio inossidabile, vetro e luce al neon, oppure di prendere posto sulla terrazza da cui possono godere di una splendida vista sul mare.

Fabio Maria Ceccarelli

Corso Due Giugno, 46
60019 Senigallia AN
Italy

Photos courtesy La Madonnina Del Pescatore

La Madonnina del Pescatore

Lungomare Italia, 11
Marzocca di Senigallia
60019 Senigallia
Italy
www.madonninadelpescatore.it

Near the Formula 1 Casino, the Pacific Restaurant joins "Male and Female", "Hard and Soft" with materials such as raw steel and silk, wood and wool. The space is functional and flexible and plays with minimal light effects, transparent materials and variable views from the inside and of the outside.

Nahe dem Formel-1-Casino gelegen, vereint das Restaurant Pacific „Männliches und Weibliches", „Hartes und Weiches" mit Materialien wie Rohstahl und Seide, Holz und Wolle. Der Raum ist funktionell flexibel und spielt mit minimalen Lichteffekten, transparenten Stoffen und variablen Ein- und Ausblicken.

Situé prés du Casino Formel 1, le restaurant Pacific associe le « masculin au féminin », le « solide au doux » au moyen de matériaux comme l'acier brut et la soie, le bois et la laine. L'espace est d'une flexibilité fonctionnelle et joue avec des effets d'éclairage réduits, des tissus transparents et la possibilité de moduler les perspectives.

Cerca del Casino Fórmula 1, el Restaurante Pacific une "lo masculino y lo femenino", "lo duro y lo blando" con materiales como el acero grueso y la seda, la madera y la lana. El espacio es flexible de modo funcional y juega con efectos mínimos de luces, materiales transparentes y vistas variables hacia dentro y hacia fuera.

Ubicato nelle vicinanze del Formel-1-Casino, il ristorante Pacific coniuga "femminile e maschile", linee "dure e morbide" grazie alla scelta di materiali quali l'acciaio grezzo e la seta, il legno e la lana. L'ambiente è polifunzionale e caratterizzato da sottili contrasti luminosi nonché giochi di trasparenze e semitrasparenze.

Studio Delrosso

Via Italia, 38
13900 Biella
Italy
www.studiodelrosso.com

Photos by Matteo Piazza

Pacific

17, Avenue des Spélugues, Monte Carlo
MC 98000
Monaco
www.pacific-restaurants.com

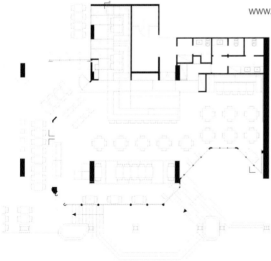

The challenge was the tight space that was available. However, by a clever arrangement of the kitchen and guest room as well as monochrome color surfaces, the restaurant on the ground floor gets across a sense of space. A *Boven room* on the first floor enables guests to retreat into a private atmosphere.

Die Herausforderung war der knappe Raum, der zur Verfügung stand. Durch geschickte Anordnung von Küche und Gastraum sowie monochromen Farbflächen vermittelt das Restaurant im Erdgeschoss dennoch einen Eindruck von Größe. Eine *Bovenkamer* im ersten Stock ermöglicht den Rückzug in eine private Atmosphäre.

Le défi à relever était l'exiguïté de l'espace dont on disposait. L'agencement habile de la cuisine et de la salle à manger ainsi que les surfaces monochromes donnent cependant l'impression que le restaurant situé au rez-de-chaussée est spacieux. Une *bovenkamer* au premier étage permet de se retirer dans une atmosphère privée.

El desafío era el pequeño espacio que estaba a disposición. Pero mediante una colocación inteligente de la cocina y del comedor así como por medio de las superficies de color monocromáticas el restaurante en la planta baja transmite una impresión de amplitud. Un *Bovenkamer* en la primera planta hace posible la retirada a una atmósfera privada.

La sfida maggiore era rappresentata dallo spazio ridotto a disposizione. Ciononostante, grazie all'abile disposizione di cucina ed area ricettiva nonché alle ampie superfici monocromatiche il ristorante riesce a trasmettere una sensazione di spazialità. La *bovenkamer* al primo piano consente di ritirarsi in un'atmosfera più intima.

Ontwerpwerk multidisciplinary design

Prinsestraat 37
2513 CA The Hague
Netherlands
www.ontwerpwerk.com

Photos by Marsel Loerman

Basaal

Dunne Bierkade 3
2512 BC The Hague
Netherlands
www.basaal.net

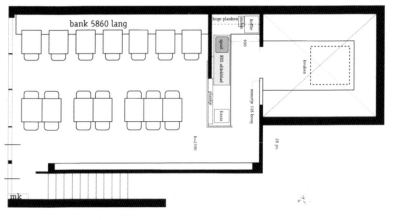

The restaurant of the Hotel Arts belongs to Barcelona's exclusive addresses along with the formalist reduction of the furnishing. Sergi Arola, the star chef works here. In 2003, he was awarded the prestigious Spanish gastronomy prize. The guests overlook the well stocked wine cellar from their tables.

Das Restaurant des Hotel Arts gehört mit der formalen Reduktion seiner Einrichtung zu den exklusiven Adressen in Barcelona. Hier wirkt Starkoch Sergi Arola, der 2003 den angesehenen spanischen Gastronomie-Preis verliehen bekam. Von den Tischen aus überblicken die Gäste das reichhaltig bestückte Weinlager.

Le restaurant de l'hôtel Arts, dont l'aménagement est caractérisé par la réduction des formes fait partie des endroits les plus raffinés de Barcelone. C'est ici que travaille le cuisinier très en vue Sergi Arola, qui a reçu en 2003 le prix renommé de la gastronomie espagnole. Les convives depuis leurs places ont une vue sur la cave très bien fournie.

El restaurante del Hotel Arts pertenece, con la reducción formal de su decoración, a las direcciones exclusivas en Barcelona. Aquí destaca el cocinero estrella Sergi Arola, quien en 2003 recibió el apreciado premio español de gastronomía. Desde las mesas los clientes divisan la abundante bodega.

Il ristorante dell'hotel Arts, caratterizzato dalla formale riduzione del suo arredamento, è tra i locali più esclusivi del momento a Barcellona. È qui che è all'opera lo chef d'eccezione Sergio Arola che nel 2003 ha vinto il prestigioso premio gastronomico spagnolo. Dai loro tavoli gli ospiti possono godere di vista sulla cantina ben fornita.

gca arquitectes associats

Calle Valencia, 289
08009 Barcelona
Spain
www.gcaarq.com

Photos courtesy Ritz Carlton PR

Arola

Hotel Arts
Carrer de la Marina, 19-21
08005 Barcelona
Spain
www.hotelartsbarcelona.com

The Lupino, a restaurant, bar and café all in one, is a room space in the shape of a pipe, whose individually, clearly defined zones flow into one another. With its two entrances and a length of 50 meters, the restaurant becomes a passage-way and the impressively lit blue, synthetic resin walkway turns into a catwalk.

Das Lupino, Restaurant, Bar und Café in einem, ist ein röhrenartiges Raumgefüge, dessen einzelne, klar definierte Zonen fließend ineinander übergehen. Mit zwei Eingängen und 50 Metern Länge wird das Restaurant zu einer Passage, der eindrucksvoll beleuchtete blaue Kunstharz-Durchgang zum Laufsteg.

Le Lupino, à la fois restaurant, bar et café a une structure d'espace tubulaire avec des zones différentes clairement définies, dont la transition de l'une à l'autre se fait aisément. Avec deux entrées et une longueur de 50 mètres, le restaurant devient un passage, la galerie en résine bleue remarquablement éclairée un podium.

El Lupino, restaurante, bar y café en uno, es una estructura tubular donde cada una de sus zonas, claramente definidas, transitan con fluidez las unas en las otras. Con dos entradas y 50 metros de longitud, el restaurante se convierte en un pasaje, el pasadizo azul de resina artificial, iluminado de forma impresionante, en una pasarela.

Il Lupino, contemporaneamente ristorante, bar e caffè, è ubicato in una struttura a galleria le cui zone singole ben riconoscibili confluiscono l'una nell'altra. Due entrate e 50 m di lunghezza conferiscono al ristorante l'aspetto di una galleria, passaggio in resina sintetica blu con illuminazione d'effetto che precede la passerella di moda.

studio nex
Ellen Rapelius, Xavier Franquesa
Calle Brusi 18, 1-1

08006 Barcelona
Spain
www.stnex.com

Photos by Nuria Rius, Oscar Brito, Marco Pastori

Lupino Lounge Restaurant

Carrer del Carme, 33
08001 Barcelona
Spain
www.lupinorestaurant.com

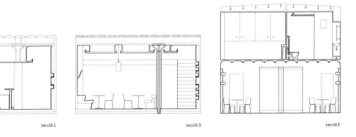

secció C   secció D   secció E

Berns Hotel in Stockholm offers a unique combination of Belle Époque, inspiring atmosphere and modern accents. Terence Conran designed the hotel's elegant and new spacious bar area and made a trend-setting, gastronomy experience out of a classic Stockholm restaurant.

Berns Hotel in Stockholm bietet eine einzigartige Kombination aus Belle Epoque, inspirierender Atmosphäre und modernen Akzenten. Terence Conran gestaltete den eleganten und großzügigen Bar-Bereich des Hotels neu und schuf aus einem klassischen Stockholmer Restaurant eine Trend setzende Erlebnisgastronomie.

L'hôtel Bern à Stockholm propose une ambiance unique combinant le style Belle Epoque, une atmosphère inspirée et des accents modernes. Terence Conran a réaménagé le vaste espace bar de l'hôtel avec élégance et a fait d'un restaurant classique de Stockholm un des lieux gastronomiques à la mode.

El Berns Hotel en Estocolmo ofrece una combinación única de Belle Epoque, una atmósfera inspiradora y acentos modernos. Terence Conran rediseñó el elegante y amplio recinto del bar en el hotel y de un clásico restaurante de Estocolmo creó una gastronomía de experiencias que marca pautas.

L'hotel Berns di Stoccolma presenta una singolare combinazione di Belle Epoque, ispirazione e modernità. A Terence Conran si deve l'ammodernamento dell'ampia ed elegante area bar dell'hotel e la trasformazione di un tipico ristorante classico di Stoccolma in una location d'eccellenza dell'avanguardia gastronomica.

Conran & Partners

22 Shad Thames
London
SE1 2YU
UK
www.conranandpartners.com

Photos courtesy Conran & Partners

Berns Hotel

Berzelii Park, PO Box 16340
103 27 Stockholm
Sweden
www.berns.se

Part of the design concept is the need to see and be seen. At the heart of design is the play with transparency, inside and transitory views. The asymmetrical seating in purple leather forms a connecting element. The furnishing is a symbol for the whole architecture—it is just as multi-functional as the room itself.

Sehen und Gesehenwerden ist Bestandteil des Konzepts, Kern der Gestaltung ist das Spiel mit Transparenz, Ein- und Durchblicken. Verbindendes Element sind die asymmetrischen Sitzmöbel in lila Leder. Die Ausstattung ist ein Symbol für die gesamte Architektur – sie ist genauso multifunktional wie der Raum selbst.

Voir et être vu est l'élément principal du concept, le point central de l'aménagement est le jeu avec la transparence, les regards sortent et entrent. Les sièges asymétriques en cuir lilas jouent le rôle d'élément de liaison. L'agencement symbolise l'architecture générale du lieu, elle est tout aussi multifonctionnelle que l'espace lui-même.

Ver y dejarse ver es la parte esencial del plan, el núcleo de la configuración es e juego con la transparencia, el ver y entrever. El elemento de unión son los asientos asimétricos de cuero lila. El equipamiento es un símbolo de toda la arquitectura: es tan multi-funcional como el espacio mismo.

Vedere ed essere visti è parte integrante della concezione architettonica, elemento predominante dell'arredamento è il gioco di trasparenze e semitrasparenze L'elemento di collegamento è rappresentato dalle poltrone asimmetriche in pelle lilla. L'arredamento riflette emblematicamente la concezione architettonica polifunzionale come l'ambiente che lo ospita.

Grego + Smolenicky Architektur GmbH

Sihlstrasse 59
8001 Zurich
Switzerland
www.grego-smolenicky.ch

Photos by Walter Mair

PIÙ

Bahnhofstrasse 25
8001 Zurich
Switzerland
www.strozzis.ch

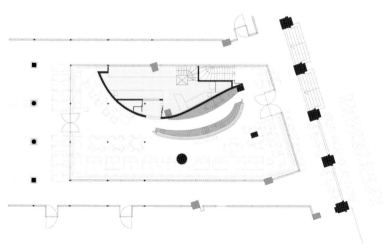

Glass walls with backlighting, metal and simple furniture mean that the Hotel restaurant is a clear contrast to the traditional Mexican architecture of One&Only Palmilla. On the peninsular Baja California, where desert and ocean meet, Tihany's urban design sets the tone with a surprise element.

Hinterleuchtete Glaswände, Metall und eine schlichte Möblierung setzen das Hotelrestaurant in einen augenscheinlichen Kontrast zur traditionellen mexikanischen Architektur des One&Only Palmilla. Auf der Halbinsel Baja California – wo Wüste und Ozean zusammentreffen – setzt Tihanys urbane Gestaltung einen Akzent mit Überraschungseffekt.

Avec des murs de verre éclairés par l'arrière, de l'acier et un mobilier sobre, l'hôtel restaurant se trouve en contraste évident avec l'architecture traditionnelle mexicaine d'One&Only Pamilla. Sur la presqu'île de Basse Californie, où désert et océan se rencontrent, la conception urbaine de l'architecte Adam D. Tihany met l'accent sur effet de surprise.

Las paredes de vidrio iluminadas por detrás, el metal y un mobiliario sencillo ponen el hotel restaurante a primera vista en contraste con la arquitectura mexicana tradicional del One&Only Palmilla. En la Península de la Baja California –donde el desierto y el océano se encuentran– la creación urbana de Tihany marca una pauta con efecto sorpresa.

Vetrate a tutta parete illuminate da dietro, metallo ed un mobilio semplice creano un evidente contrasto con l'architettura messicana tradizionale dell'One&Only Palmilla. Nella penisola Baja California – là dove deserto ed oceano si congiungono – l'arredamento cittadino di Tihanys crea una nuova tendenza non scevra di effetto sorpresa.

Tihany Design
Adam D. Tihany, Rafael Alvarez, Peter K. Lu, Julie Frank

135 West 27th Street
New York, NY 10001
USA
www.tihanydesign.com

Photos by Andrea Martiradonna

C

One&Only Palmilla Km 7.5 Carretera Transpeninsular
23400 San Jose del Cabo
Mexico
www.oneandonlyresorts.com

The restaurant and bar that is part of a tennis and fitness club form a unit, with standing and seating room loosely mixed together. The glass walls are reminiscent of a steamed-up shower cabinet, the wood is used to imitate the sport equipment and the flooring is styled on mats in the changing rooms.

Das einem Tennis- und Fitnessclub angeschlossene Restaurant und seine Bar bildet eine Einheit, Steh- und Sitzplätze sind locker gemischt. Die Glaswände erinnern an von Dampf beschlagene Duschwände, das verwendete Holz ist dem der Sportgeräte und der Boden den Fußmatten in Umkleideräumen nachgebildet.

Contigus à un club de tennis et de sport, le restaurant et son bar forment une unité, il n'y a pas de limite nette entre les places assises et les places debout. Les cloisons de verre rappellent les parois embuées d'une douche, le bois utilisé est semblable à celui des équipements sportifs et le sol reproduit celui des nattes des cabines.

El restaurante –anexado a un gimnasio y club de tenis– y su bar conforman una unidad, los asientos y los sitios para estar de pie están mezclados libremente. Las paredes de vidrio recuerdan a las paredes empañadas de una ducha, la madera empleada imita la de los aparatos para el deporte y el suelo las esteras en los vestuarios.

Il ristorante ed il bar annessi ad un tennis club e alla palestra formano un tutt'uno armonioso in cui posti in piedi e a sedere sono distribuiti senza ubbidire ad una disposizione fissa. Le pareti in vetro ricordano le pareti delle docce appannate dal vapore, il legno impiegato è una riproposta del legno degli attrezzi sportivi, il pavimento infine è una copia dei tappetini degli spogliatoi.

Dodd Mitchell Design Associates

8336 West 3rd Street
Los Angeles, CA 90048
USA
www.doddmitchell.com

Photos by Martin Nicholas Kunz

Oliver Café

9601 Wilshire Boulevard / Camden
Beverly Hills, CA 90210
USA
www.olivercafe.com

The intricately designed restaurant and bar is located in the MGM Grand Hotel. The glinting metallic cylinder is full of high-tech and light effects and is striking for its mundane elegance: stainless steel polished like a mirror, polished walnut and Ferrari red leather furnishing throughout.

Im MGM Grand Hotel befindet sich das aufwendig gestaltete Restaurant mit einer Bar. Der metallisch schillernde Zylinder steckt voller Hightech und Lichteffekten und besticht durch mondäne Eleganz: auf Spiegelglanz polierter Edelstahl, poliertes Walnussholz und eine durchgehend Ferrari-rote Lederausstattung.

C'est dans l'hôtel MGM que se trouve le restaurant avec bar luxueusement agencé. Le cylindre aux reflets métalliques chatoyants est rempli de high-tech et d'effets de lumière et séduit par son élégance mondaine : de l'acier poli comme du miroir, du noyer poli et un agencement général en cuir rouge Ferrari.

En el MGM Grand Hotel se encuentra el restaurante con bar configurado lujosamente. El cilindro irisado metálicamente está lleno de efectos de luz y de alta tecnología y cautiva por su elegancia mundana: acero noble pulido brillante como un espejo, madera de nogal pulida y una decoración constante de cuero rojo Ferrari.

Nel Grand Hotel MGM si trova un ristorante con bar di ambizioso progetto. Il cilindro dai riflessi metallici cangianti colpisce per la ricchezza di particolari hightech e per i giochi di luce oltre che per la sua eleganza mondana: acciaio inossidabile tirato a lucido, legno di noce lucidato ed un ricorrente richiamo cromatico rappresentato dagli interni rosso Ferrari in pelle.

Tihany Design
Adam D. Tihany, Carolyn Ament, Paris Forino, Peter K. Lu

135 West 27th Street
New York, NY 10001
USA
www.tihanydesign.com

Photos by Eric Laignel

Teatro

MGM Grand Hotel & Casino
3799 Las Vegas Boulevard South
Las Vegas, NV 89109
USA

There are plenty of grill restaurants in Koreatown, but none is designed as impressively as this one. The design is based on open and enclosed spaces and has impressive, curved walls and ceilings made out of bamboo. The restaurant is dominated by stainless steel that has been worked into sculpture-like forms.

In Koreatown gibt es eine Fülle von Grillrestaurants, aber keines ist so eindrucksvoll gestaltet wie dieses. Die Gestaltung beruht auf offenen und geschlossenen Räumen und beeindruckt durch seine gewölbten Wänden und Decken aus Bambusholz. Dominiert wir das Restaurant durch skulpturengleich verarbeiteten Edelstahl.

Dans le quartier de Koreatown, il y a une foule de restaurants grills, mais aucun n'est aménagé de façon aussi impressionnante que celui-là. La conception repose sur l'aménagement des espaces ouverts et fermés et les murs et des plafonds voûtés en bambou qui produisent une forte impression. L'acier travaillé comme des sculptures est un élément dominant dans le restaurant.

En Corea Town hay una gran cantidad de restaurantes de carnes a la parrilla pero ninguno está creado de forma tan impresionante como éste. El diseño se basa en los espacios abiertos y cerrados e impresiona por las paredes arqueadas y los techos de madera de bambú. El restaurante está dominado por el acero fino trabajado como esculturas.

A Koreatown c'è una moltitudine di grill rooms ma nessuno è arredato in modo così d'effetto come questo. La realizzazione è particolarmente riuscita grazie alla fluidità di spazi aperti e chiusi e grazie alle pareti e ai soffitti arrotondati in legno di bambù. L'acciaio inossidabile è il materiale predominante lavorato ad effetto scultura.

studio rcl
Richard Cutts Lundquist

1257 Vista Court
Glendale, CA 91205
USA
www.rcl.net

Photos by Mark Luthringer, Benny Chan

Chosun Galbee

3330 W. Olympic Boulevard
Los Angeles, CA 90010
USA
www.chosungalbee.com

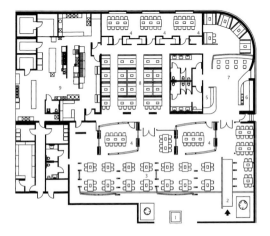

The Eurochow is housed in a historic building in Los Angeles. All the ceilings were removed in the former bank building, in order to integrate a tall, white, marble obelisk. The color white dominates the room and the furnishing is also kept white and skillfully integrated, as well as the open show kitchen.

Das Eurochow ist in einem historischen Gebäude in Los Angeles untergebracht. In dem ehemaligen Bankgebäude wurden alle Decken entfernt, um einen hohen weißen Marmorobelisk zu integrieren. Weiße Farbe dominiert den Raum, eine ebenfalls in Weiß gehaltene Möblierung sowie eine offene Showküche sind gekonnt integriert.

Le restaurant Eurochow est aménagé dans un bâtiment historique de Los Angeles. Dans l'ancien immeuble de banque, on a enlevé tous les plafonds pour intégrer un grand obélisque de marbre blanc. Le blanc domine l'espace, un mobilier également blanc ainsi qu'une cuisine ouverte y sont habilement intégrés.

El Eurochow está alojado en un edificio histórico en Los Angeles. En el antiguo edificio de un banco se retiraron todos los techos para integrar un alto obelisco de mármol blanco. El color blanco domina el espacio, un mobiliario también en blanco, así como una cocina-espectáculo abierta están integrados de un modo muy bien conseguido.

L'Eurochow è situato in un edificio storico di Los Angeles, un ex istituto bancario ristrutturato nel quale tutti i soffitti sono stati rimossi per far posto ad un alto obelisco di marmo bianco. Il colore bianco è la nota predominante dell'arredamento, caratterizzato altresì da complementi d'arredo in bianco e da una cucina show cooking che si armonizzano perfettamente con l'ambiente.

Michael Chow Design Group

9538 Brighton Way St. 316
Beverly Hills, CA 90210
USA
www.mrchow.com

Photos by Martin Nicholas Kunz

Eurochow

1099 Westwood Boulevard
Los Angeles, CA 90024
USA
www.eurochow.com

Here, the minimalist style of an austere room was crossed with deliberately elegant simplicity. In this Vietnamese restaurant there is only Pho, a popular noodle soup. If everything fits well together, as it does here, then even something relatively unspectacular can quickly become a favorite with the regular customers.

Hier wurde der Minimalismus eines kargen Raums mit einer bewusst eingesetzten eleganten Schlichtheit gekreuzt. In diesem vietnamesischen Restaurant gibt es nur Pho, eine beliebte Nudelsuppe. Wenn wie hier alles zusammenpasst, avanciert auch Unspektakuläres schnell zum Szeneliebling.

Le minimalisme d'un espace sobre rencontre ici l'élégante simplicité pour laquelle on a ici opté délibérément. Dans ce restaurant vietnamien, on ne mange que Pho, une soupe de nouilles très appréciée. Quand comme ici tout s'accorde bien, un endroit banal devient vite un des favoris.

Aquí el minimalismo de un espacio pobre fue cruzado con una elegante sencillez empleada conscientemente. En este restaurante vietnamita sólo hay pho, una apreciada sopa de pasta. Cuando, como aquí, todo armoniza, lo espectacular asciende rápidamente a convertirse en lo favorito de la movida.

La scelta di un'elegante semplicità nell'arredamento è stata dettata dalla frugalità dell'ambiente di questo ristorante vietnamese in qui si serve solo la Pho, una popolare minestra a base di pasta. Quando tutti i dettagli si sposano così bene, anche l'insieme meno spettacolare può diventare in breve tempo un famoso locale alla moda.

Escher GuneWardena Architecture

815 Silver Lake Boulevard
Los Angeles, CA 90026
USA
www.egarch.net

Photos by Martin Nicholas Kunz

Pho Café

2841 West Sunset Boulevard
Los Angeles, CA 90026
USA

The tiles, walls and furnishings are kept in yellow tones that are adapted to each other. The restaurant is reminiscent of American 1970s design and offers a wealth of contrasts with the concave form of the ceiling elements and handmade wallpaper.

Fliesen, Wände und Einrichtungen sind in aufeinander abgestimmten Gelbtönen gehalten. Zusammen mit den konkav geformten Deckenelementen und den handgefertigten Tapeten bietet das Restaurant eine Fülle an Kontrasten und erinnert an amerikanisches Design der 70er Jahre.

Les carrelages, les murs et l'aménagement sont dans des tons jaunes qui s'accordent les uns avec les autres. Les éléments concaves du plafond et les tapis faits main confèrent au restaurant une ambiance pleine de contrastes et rappelle le design américain des années soixante-dix.

Las baldosas, las paredes y los equipamientos están en tonos amarillos que armonizan unos con otros. Junto con los elementos del techo de forma cóncava y los papeles pintados hechos a mano, el restaurante ofrece una gran cantidad de contrastes y recuerda al diseño americano de los años 70.

L'effetto di pavimenti, pareti e complementi d'arredo gioca sull'armoniosa gamma cromatica di sfumature solari. Gli elementi concavi del soffitto e le tappezzerie realizzate a mano danno vita, insieme agli effetti cromatici, ad un insieme ricco di contrasti che ha molto del design americano degli anni Settanta.

Koning Eizenberg Architecture

1454 25th Street
Santa Monica, CA 90404
USA
www.kearch.com

Photos by Martin Nicholas Kunz

The Standard Downtown

550 South Flower Street
Los Angeles, CA 90069
USA
www.standardhotel.com

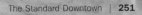

An integrated café area was created along with a Take-Away restaurant. Walls and partitions in the café area are suspended from the ceiling in a steel frame and filled in with corrugated cardboard, assembled as strips and held in by pressure. An eye-catcher is a wall with 479 different coffee cup lids that were set in plaster.

Zusammen mit einem Take-away-Restaurant entstand ein integrierter Café-Bereich. Wände und Abtrennungen dieses Café-Bereiches sind in einem Stahlrahmen von der Decke abgehängt und mit Streifen aus geschichteter Wellpappe ausgefüllt, die durch Druck zusammengehalten werden. Blickfang ist eine Wand mit 479 unterschiedlichen „coffee-cup"-Deckeln, die in Gips verewigt wurden.

On a créé un restaurant de plats à emporter dans lequel on a intégré un espace café. Les murs et cloisons de cet espace café sont suspendus au plafond dans un châssis en acier et remplis de lanières de carton ondulé empilées, le tout étant maintenu par pression. Le point de mire est le mur avec les 479 couvercles de tasses de café différents, qui sont immortalisés dans le plâtre.

Junto con un restaurante de comidas para llevar surgió un recinto de café integrado. Las paredes y separaciones de este recinto de café están colgadas del techo en un marco de acero y rellenas de tiras de cartón ondulado en capas que se mantienen unidas a presión. El centro de atención es una pared con 479 tapaderas distintas de tazas de café perpetuadas en yeso.

Insieme al ristorante take-away è stata creata un'area pausa caffè. Pareti e divisori di quest'area, come incorniciati in un profilo d'acciaio, pendono giù dal soffitto e sono rivestiti di cartone ondulato multistrato compresso a strisce. Di grande effetto visivo sono i 479 coperchietti di diversa foggia dei bicchieri da caffè da portar via che il gesso ha immortalato lungo un'intera parete.

Lewis.Tsurumaki.Lewis LTL architects

147 Essex Street
New York, NY 10002
USA
www.ltlwork.net

Photos by Michael Moran

Ini Ani Coffee Shop

105 Stanton Street
New York, NY 10002
USA
www.iniani.com

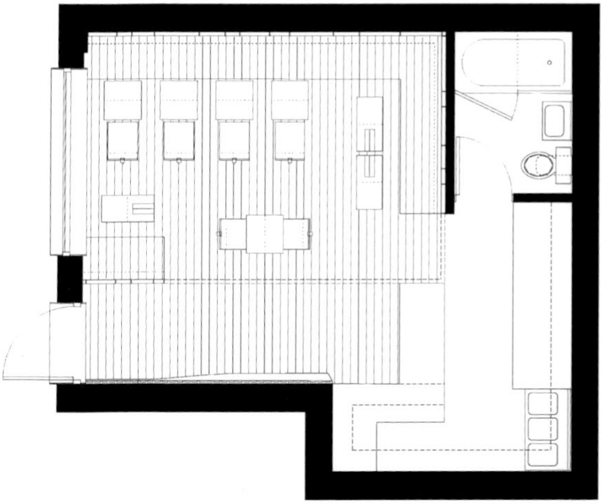

Andre Kikoski drew inspiration for the furnishing from his impressions of the Spanish Alhambra and Fellini's classic film "La Dolce Vita". The restaurant, which is located in a 1909 building, extends over several stories. The challenge was to create drama in the transitions from the old and new building.

Bei der Einrichtung hat sich Andre Kikoski von Eindrücken der spanischen Alhambra und Fellinis Filmklassiker „La Dolce Vita" inspirieren lassen. Das Restaurant, das in einem Gebäude von 1909 untergebracht ist, erstreckt sich über mehrere Stockwerke. Die Herausforderung war, Übergänge von Alt- und Neubau zu dramatisieren.

Pour l'aménagement Andre Kikoski s'est inspiré d'impressions de l'Alhambra espagnol et du film « La Dolce Vita », grand classique de Fellini. Le restaurant, situé dans un bâtiment de 1909 s'étend sur plusieurs étages. Le défi ici consistait à mettre en scène les transitions entre l'ancien et le nouveau bâtiment.

En la decoración Andre Kikoski se dejó inspirar por impresiones de la Alhambra española y del clásico del cine de Fellini, "La Dolce Vita". El restaurante, que está alojado en un edificio de 1909, se extiende por varias plantas. El desafío era dramatizar los pasos entre el edificio antiguo y el nuevo.

Per l'arredamento Andre Kikoski si è ispirato alle atmosfere dell'Alhambra spagnola e ad un grande classico di Fellini, "La Dolce Vita". Il ristorante, ubicato in un edificio del 1909, si dispone su più piani. L'armonizzazione fluida fra vecchio e nuovo ha costituito la sfida architettonica maggiore.

Andre Kikoski AIA

180 Varick Street, Suite 1316
New York, NY 10014
USA
www.akarchitect.com

Photos by Peter Aaron / Esto

Suba

109 Ludlow Street
New York, NY 10002
USA
www.subanyc.com

The Cantinella is a modern interpretation of an Italian wine shop. The furnishing is influenced by built-in elements of solid nut wood (used for wine barrels) as well as blackened steel (used for barrel rings) and complemented by handmade silk lights and modernist *trompe-l'œil* art.

Das Cantinella ist eine moderne Interpretation eines italienischen Weingeschäftes. Die Einrichtung wird geprägt durch Einbauten aus massivem Nussbaum (Fassholz) sowie geschwärztem Stahl (Fassring) und ergänzt durch handgefertigte Leuchten aus Seide und eine modernistische Trompe-l'Œil-Malerei.

La Cantinella est une version moderne d'un magasin de vins italien. L'aménagement est caractérisé par des éléments intégrés en noyer massif (bois de tonneau) ainsi qu'en acier noirci (cercle du tonneau) et est complété par des lampes artisanales en soie et une peinture en trompe-l'œil moderniste.

El Cantinella es una interpretación moderna de una vinatería italiana. La instalación se caracteriza por los módulos de madera masiva de nogal (madera de barril) así como por el acero ennegrecido (anilla de barril) y es completada por lámparas de seda, hechas a mano, y una pintura *trompe-l'œil* modernista.

La Cantinella rappresenta una versione moderna di enoteca all'italiana. L'arredamento è caratterizzato da mobili ad incasso in noce massiccio (legname per botti) nonché da acciaio brunito (cerchio della botte) ed è completato perfettamente da lampade di seta realizzate a mano e da moderne pitture trompe-l'œil.

Lynch / Eisinger / Design (L/E/D)

224 Centre Street, Fifth Floor
New York, NY 10013
USA
www.lyncheisingerdesign.com

Photos by Amy Barkow, courtesy Lynch / Eisinger / Design

The Cantinella

23 Avenue A
New York, NY 10009
USA
www.cantinella.com

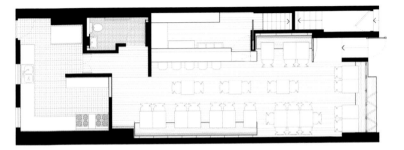

You enter the two-storey restaurant by the lobby of the Chambers A Hotel. The gallery is the attraction, since it arches over part of the main restaurant below and interrupts the hall-like character of the room. Low-key earth and wood tones additionally ensure pleasant, diffused lighting.

Über die Lobby des Chambers A Hotels gelangt man in das zweistöckige Restaurant. Anziehungspunkt ist die Galerie, die einen Teil des darunter liegenden Hauptrestaurants überdeckt und so den Hallencharakter des Raumes unterbricht. Dezente Erd- und Holztöne sorgen zudem für angenehm diffuse Lichtverhältnisse.

Au-dessus du hall de l'hôtel Chambers A, on accède à un restaurant de deux étages. Le point d'attraction est la galerie, qui recouvre une partie du restaurant situé en dessous et interrompt ainsi le caractère de hall de la pièce. Des tons terre et bois discrets contribuent de surcroît à créer une agréable ambiance de lumière diffuse.

Por el lobby del Chambers A Hotel se llega al restaurante de dos plantas. El punto de atracción es la galería que cubre una parte del restaurante principal situado debajo interrumpiendo de esta manera el carácter de hall de la sala. Los tonos decentes y de madera proporcionan además unas condiciones de luz agradablemente difusas.

Attraverso la lobby dell'hotel Chambers A è possibile accedere al ristorante a due piani. Un punto di grande attrazione è costituito dalla galleria che copre parte del ristorante principale sottostante e che interrompe la spazialità aperta dell'ambiente. Inoltre piacevoli giochi di luce diffusa sono il risultato delle smorzate tonalità della terra e del legno.

Rockwell Group

5 Union Square West
New York, NY 10003
USA
www.rockwellgroup.com

Photos by David Joseph, courtesy Rockwell Group

Town Restaurant

Chambers A Hotel
15 West 56th Street
New York, NY 10019
USA
www.townnyc.com

This restaurant takes its name from the small, private "gondolas" (Pods) that the architects included. Ergonomic curves dominate in the retro-futuristic room. David Rockwell was inspired with his extravagant design by films like "The Sleeper" and "2001: Space Odyssey".

Namensgeber sind die kleinen, privaten „Gondeln" (Pods), die die Architekten in das Restaurant eingefügt haben. In dem retro-futuristischen Raum dominieren ergonomische Kurven, bei der extravaganten Gestaltung hat sich David Rockwell von den Filmen „The Sleeper" und „2001: Space Odyssey" beeinflussen lassen.

Le nom vient des petites cabines (pods) privées que les architectes ont intégrées dans le restaurant. Dans l'espace rétro-futuriste, les courbes ergonomiques dominent. Ce sont les films « Sleeper » et « 2001, Odyssée de l'espace » qui ont influencé David Rockwell pour cette conception extravagante.

El nombre se lo dieron las pequeñas "góndolas" privadas (Pods) que los arquitectos agregaron al restaurante. En la sala retro-futurista dominan las curvas ergonómicas, para el extravagante diseño David Rockwell se dejó inspirar por las películas "El durmiente" y "2001: Odisea del espacio".

Il ristorante prende il nome dalle piccole gondole private (Pods) che gli architetti hanno voluto far confluire nell'arredamento del ristorante. In un ambiente retrofuturistico predominano linee arrotondate ergonomiche, un tocco stravagante per il quale David Rockwell si è ispirato ai film "Il dormiglione" e "2001: Odissea nello spazio".

Rockwell Group

5 Union Square West
New York, NY 10003
USA
www.rockwellgroup.com

Photos by Paul Warchol, courtesy Rockwell Group

Pod Restaurant

3636 Sansom St
Philadelphia, PA 19104
USA

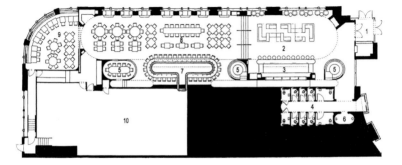

The luxury restaurant designed by André Putman is characterized by subtle forms. From the street, you enter a romantic inner courtyard by an entrance gate and you actually feel a bit as if you are in Provence. The atmosphere also continues through the alternating green and pastel-colored inner rooms.

Eine unaufdringliche Gestaltung kennzeichnet das von André Putman gestaltete Nobelrestaurant. Von der Straße aus tritt man durch ein Portal in den romantischen Innenhof und fühlt sich tatsächlich ein wenig wie in der Provence. Diese Atmosphäre zieht sich auch durch die abwechselnd begrünten und pastellfarbenen Innenräume.

Un agencement discret caractérise le restaurant de grande classe qu'André Putman a aménagé. Venant de la rue, on entre par un portail dans une cour intérieure romantique et on se sent vraiment un peu comme en Provence. Cette atmosphère se poursuit aussi dans les espaces intérieurs où on trouve alternativement des plantes et des couleurs pastel.

Una configuración modesta caracteriza el restaurante de lujo creado por André Putman. Desde la calle se entra por un portal en el romántico patio y uno realmente se siente un poco como en la Provenza. Esta atmósfera se extiende también por las salas interiores alternativamente en verde y en colores pastel.

La sobrietà è l'elemento predominante dell'arredamento scelto da André Putman per questo ristorante esclusivo. Dalla strada si accede direttamente nella romantica corte interna dove si ha subito la lieve sensazione di trovarsi in Provenza. Una volta entrati, quest'atmosfera viene potenziata dall'alternarsi degli interni ammantati di verde e in colori pastello.

Andrée Putman

83, Avenue Denfert-Rochereau
75014 Paris
France
www.andreeputman.com

Photos by Martin Nicholas Kunz

Bastide

8475 Melrose Place / La Cienega Boulevard
West Hollywood, CA 90069
USA

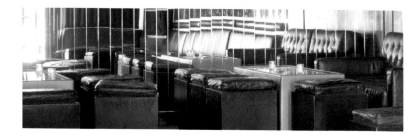

The Steakhouse on Sunset Strip certainly does not live up to the cliché for this type of restaurant. The material selection is striking: leather-lined walls alternate with lead-colored, smooth plaster-work and gray color-washed walls. The center of the restaurant is formed by a pebbled area, marked off by steel posts and brightly colored lanterns.

Das Steakhouse am Sunset Strip entspricht so gar nicht dem Klischee dieser Gattung. Bestechend ist die Materialauswahl: Mit Leder gepolsterte Wände wechseln mit beigefarbenem Glattputz und in Grau gewischten Decken. Die Lokalmitte markiert eine mit Stahlstangen und bunten Laternen abgegrenzte Kieselsteinfläche.

Le Steakhouse sur le Sunset Strip ne correspond pas du tout au cliché de ce genre de restaurant. Le choix des matériaux est séduisant : des murs recouverts de cuir alternent avec un crépi beige lisse et des plafonds peints en gris. Une surface composée de cailloux, délimitée par des rampes d'acier et des lanternes colorées, marque le centre du restaurant.

El Steakhouse en Sunset Strip no corresponde del todo al tópico de este género. La elección de materiales cautiva: Las paredes tapizadas de cuero alternan con el revoque liso de color beige y los techos difuminados en gris. El centro del local marca una superficie de guijarros delimitada por barras de acero y farolas de colores.

Questo steakhouse ubicato sul Sunset Strip rompe totalmente con l'immagine stereotipata solitamente associata a che questo tipo di locale. Affascinante la scelta dei materiali: rivestimenti di pelle imbottita alle pareti vengono alternati a intonaco liscio beige e soffitti grigi effetto lavato. Il centro del locale è costituito da una superficie acciottolata delimitata da barre in acciaio e da lanterne colorate.

Tag Front

818 S. Broadway 700
Los Angeles, CA 90014
www.tagfront.com

Photos by Martin Nicolas Kunz

Boa

8462 W. Sunset Boulevard
West Hollywood, CA 90069
USA
www.boasteak.com

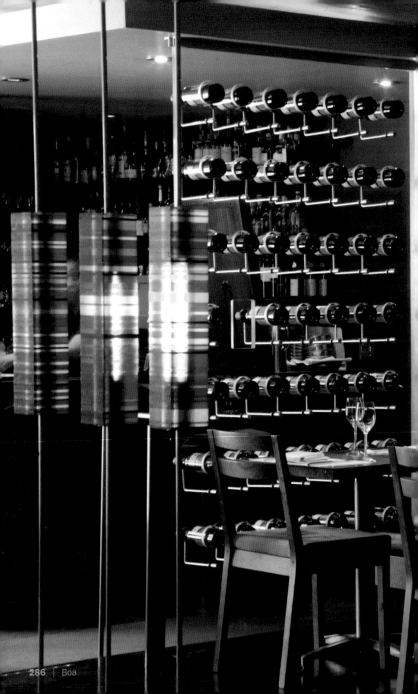

Glass balconies and window fronts, suspended over a cliff, create a unifying element between the restaurant and nature. The elegant restaurant was designed in the cool greens and blue tones of the ocean. Guests relax in comfortable seating groups or dine with a breathtaking view of the ocean.

Über einer Klippe schwebend schaffen Glasbalkone und Fensterfronten eine Einheit zwischen Restaurant und Natur. Das elegante Restaurant wurde in den kühlen grünen und blauen Farben des Ozeans gestaltet. Die Gäste entspannen in gemütlichen Sitzgruppen oder speisen mit atemberaubendem Blick auf den Ozean.

Les balcons de verres et les fenêtres, semblant flotter au-dessus d'un écueil, créent une unité entre le restaurant et la nature. L'élégant restaurant a été conçu dans les verts et les bleus froids de l'océan. Les convives se détendent agréablement en petits groupes et se restaurent en profitant d'une vue sur l'océan à couper le souffle.

Flotando sobre un arrecife, los balcones y las fachadas de vidrio crean una unidad entre el restaurante y la naturaleza. El elegante restaurante fue configurado en los colores fríos del océano verdes y azules. Los clientes se relajan en cómodos grupos de asientos o comen con vistas espectaculares al océano.

Sospesi su uno scoglio, terrazzo a vetri e facciate creano un tutt'uno senza soluzione di continuità fra il ristorante e la natura. All'interno dell'elegante ristorante vengono riproposte le tonalità fredde verdi e blu dell'oceano. Gli ospiti possono rilassarsi in comode poltrone o pasteggiare a tu per tu con l'oceano.

Lazzarini Pickering Architetti

Via Cola di Rienzo 28
00192 Rome
Italy

Tanner Architects

52 Albion Street
Surry Hills NSW 2010
Sydney
Australia
www.tannerarchitects.com.au

Photos by Matteo Piazza

Icebergs Dining Room & Bar

One Notts Avenue
Bondi Beach NSW 2026
Sydney
Australia
www.idrb.com

The Philippe Starck-designed restaurant Felix is located under the roof on the 28th and 29th floor of the traditional Peninsula hotel. It combines an imaginative cuisine with an intoxicating interior and unusual lighting—plus a breathtaking view of Hong Kong's skyline.

Unter dem Dach im 28. und 29. Stockwerk des traditionsreichen Peninsula befindet sich das von Philippe Starck gestaltete Restaurant Felix. Es verbindet einfallsreiche Küche mit einem berauschendem Interieur und einer ausgefallener Beleuchtung – plus atemberaubender Aussicht auf die Skyline von Hongkong.

Le restaurant Felix conçu par Philippe Strack se trouve au 28ième et 29ième étage, sous le toit du Peninsula riche de tradition. Il réunit une cuisine créative à un intérieur stupéfiant et un éclairage peu ordinaire, avec en plus une vue époustouflante sur l'horizon de Hongkong.

Bajo el tejado en las plantas 28 y 29 del Peninsula, de gran tradición, se halla el Restaurant Felix configurado por Philippe Starck. Une la cocina imaginativa con un interior embriagador y una iluminación extravagante además de una vista impresionante hacia la skyline de Hongkong.

Nel sottotetto, al 28simo e 29simo piano della Peninsula così ricca di tradizioni, è ubicato il ristorante Felix, opera di Philippe Starck. Gli ingredienti di successo sono una cucina fantasiosa, interni da capogiro ed un'illuminazione originale a cui si aggiunge la vista mozzafiato sulla *Skyline* di Hong Kong.

Philippe Starck Network

18/20, Rue du Faubourg du Temple
75011 Paris
France
www.philippe-starck.com

Photos by Martin Nicholas Kunz

Felix

The Peninsula Hotel
Salisbury Road, Kowloon
Hong Kong
www.hongkong.peninsula.com

Cyberport opened Le Meridien as Hong Kong's most modern hotel of the moment. The open restaurant in the lobby is impressive due to the opaque lights, which are the height of room, the subdued colors, as well as room partitions of translucent gauze. A bar is illuminated with diffused light and inviting armchairs in the palm garden create an oasis of calm.

Mit dem Le Meridien Cyberport eröffnete in Hongkong das derzeit modernste Hotel. Das offene Restaurant in der Lobby beeindruckt durch raumhohe opake Leuchten, gedämpfte Farben sowie Raumtrennungen aus transluzider Gaze. Eine diffus beleuchtete Theke und einladende Sessel im Palmengarten schaffen eine Oase der Ruhe.

Avec le Meridien Cyberport, c'est l'hôtel le plus moderne qui s'est ouvert à Hong-kong. Le restaurant ouvert sur le hall impressionne par des luminaires opaques qui montent jusqu'au plafond, des couleurs estompées ainsi que par des cloisons de gaze translucide qui séparent les espaces. Un bar éclairé d'une lumière diffuse et des sièges accueillants créent dans le jardin de palmiers un oasis de paix.

Con Le Meridien, Cyberport abrió en Hongkong el hotel más moderno actualmente. El restaurante abierto en el lobby impresiona con las luces opacas de la altura de la sala, los colores apagados así como las separaciones del espacio de gasa translúcida. Un mostrador iluminado difusamente y sillones invitando en el jardín de palmeras crean un oasis de tranquilidad.

L'hotel Le Meridien Cyberport rappresenta l'esempio più moderno di architettura alberghiera finora realizzato ad Hong Kong. Il ristorante aperto situato nella lobby dell'hotel colpisce soprattutto per le lampade opache a tutta parete, i colori tenui nonché i divisori in garza semitrasparente. Il bancone bar, immerso nella luce diffusa, e le poltrone invitanti del giardino delle palme contribuiscono a creare un'atmosfera da oasi di pace.

Arquitectonica

1114 West 26th Street
New York, NY 10001
USA
www.arquitectonica.com

Photos by Martin Nicholas Kunz

Umami

Le Meridien Cyberport
100 Cyberport Road
Hong Kong
www.hongkong.lemeridien.com

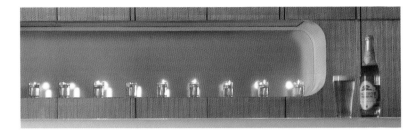

Senso in Delhi, India, is divided into a bar and an Italian restaurant. The furnishing by Rajiv Saini is mainly kept in white. There is not a trace of typical Indian folklore and epoxy resin, synthetic leather, glass, white flowers, white candles and restrained neon colors dominate.

Das Senso im indischen Dehli ist aufgeteilt in eine Bar und in ein italienisches Restaurant. Die Einrichtung ist von Rajiv Saini überwiegend in Weiß gehalten worden. Keine Spur von typisch indischer Folklore, es dominieren Epoxidharz, Kunstleder, Glas, weiße Blumen, weiße Kerzen und dezent eingesetzte Neonfarben.

Le Senso, situé à Delhi en Inde, est partagé en un bar et un restaurant. Rajiv Saini a conçu un aménagement presque tout blanc. Aucune trace de folklore indien, ce sont ici la résine époxyde, le cuir synthétique, le verre, des fleurs blanches, des bougies blanches et les discrètes couleurs des néons qui dominent.

El Senso en la india Delhi está dividido en un bar y un restaurante italiano. La decoración es de Rajiv Saini predominantemente en blanco. No hay ni una huella de folklore típico indio, dominan la resina epoxi, el cuero artificial, el vidrio, las flores blancas, las velas blancas y los colores de neón empleados de forma decente.

Il ristorante Senso, nella città indiana di Delhi, è suddiviso in bar ed in ristorante italiano. L'arredamento scelto volutamente da Rajiv Saini è prevalentemente bianco. Al posto del folklore indiano, di cui non vi è alcuna traccia, predominano resina epossidica, similpelle, vetro, fiori bianchi, candele bianche e colori al neon impiegati con sobrietà.

Rajiv Saini + Associates

23, Surya Kiran, Khar West
Mumbai - 400 052
India

Photos by Martin Nicholas Kunz

Senso Bar & Restaurant

33 Basant Lok Community
New Delhi 110001
India

The Grand Hyatt Mumbai is one of the newest hotel developments in Mumbai. The owners have introduced Italian living with the Celini Restaurant in a city shaped by contrasts. The round window at the end of the lobby is optically imposing and reminiscent of an oversized telescope with a view of the night sky.

Das Grand Hyatt Mumbai ist eine der neuesten Hotelanlagen in Mumbai. Die Betreiber haben mit dem Restaurant Celini italienische Lebensart in die von Gegensätzen geprägte Stadt gebracht. Optisch markant ist das runde Fenster am Ende der Lobby, das an ein überdimensionales Fernrohr mit Blick in den Sternenhimmel erinnert.

Le Grand Hyatt Mumbai est un des complexes hôteliers les plus récents de Mumbai. Avec le restaurant Celini, les gérants ont apporté l'art de vivre italien dans une ville pleine de contrastes. On remarque d'emblée la fenêtre ronde au bout du hall, qui fait penser à un immense télescope dirigé vers le ciel.

El Grand Hyatt Mumbai es una de las más nuevas instalaciones hoteleras en Mumbai. Con el restaurante Celini los operadores llevaron el estilo de vida italiano a la ciudad marcada por los contrastes. Visualmente característica es la ventana redonda al final del lobby que recuerda a un telescopio gigantesco con vistas al cielo estrellado.

Il Grand Hyatt Mumbai è una delle strutture alberghiere più nuove a Mumbai. Con il ristorante Celini i gestori hanno importato un pezzo di stile di vita italiano in una città segnata dalle contraddizioni. L'elemento architettonico più marcato è rappresentato dalla grande finestra rotonda, situata alla fine della lobby, dalle sembianze di un enorme telescopio puntato sul cielo stellato.

Lohan Caprile Goettsch Architects

224 South Michigan Ave., 17th Floor
CA 90802
USA
www.csrdesign.com

Chadha Siembieda Remedios

400 Oceangate, Long Beach
CA 90802
USA

Photos by Martin Nicholas Kunz

Celini

Hotel Grand Hyatt Mumbai
Off Western Express Highway
Santacruz (East)
Mumbai 400 055
India
www.mumbai.grand.hyatt.com

An attention-grabbing building with café and apartment and with a view of Hiroshima was created on a basic square design. The building is resting on supports and radically points to perspectives of how ecological needs and high-tech, which the architects call "power of nature", can be reconciled.

Mit Blick auf Hiroshima entstand ein Aufsehen erregendes Gebäude mit Café und Wohnung über einem annähernd quadratischen Grundriss. Das aufgeständerte Gebäude zeigt auf radikale Weise Perspektiven auf, wie sich ökologischer Anspruch und Hightech, den die Architekten als „power of nature" bezeichnen, versöhnen lassen.

C'est sur un plan presque carré qu'a été construit ce bâtiment sensationnel, comportant un café et un appartement et d'où on a une vue sur Hiroshima. Le bâtiment surélevé démontre de façon radicale comment les exigences écologiques et la haute technologie, que les architectes décrivent comme le « pouvoir de la nature », peuvent se concilier.

Con vistas a Hiroshima surgió, sobre una planta más o menos cuadrada, un edificio con café y vivienda que causa sensación. El edificio erigido sobre soportes muestra de forma radical las perspectivas de cómo pueden reconciliarse la pretensión ecológica y la alta tecnología que los arquitectos denominan "power of nature".

L'edificio con vista su Hiroshima (costituito da caffè ed appartamento), che al momento della sua costruzione aveva provocato parecchio scalpore, presenta una pianta quasi quadrata. L'edificio sopraelevato mostra in modo radicale come sia possibile conciliare impegno ecologico ed alta tecnologia, sposalizio che gli architetti amano definire "power of nature".

Suppose Design Office

13-2-3F, Kako-machi, Naka-ku
Hiroshima 730-0812
Japan
www.suppose.jp

Photos by Nacasa & Partners

float restaurant café

3-16 Bishamondai-2 Asaminami ward
Hiroshima730-0812
Japan

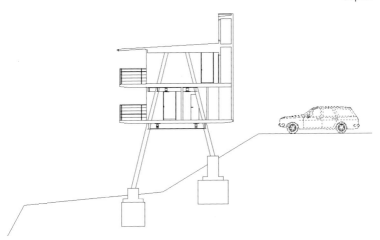

That the main theme here is the wine bar, housed in a cellar room, is evident by the interior furnishing. Stairs lead to individual, private, cave-like kind of cocoons made out of fiber glass for two to four people. These cocoons are distributed in the restaurant over several stories.

Das der Name des in einem Kellerraum untergebrachten Weinlokals hier Programm ist, offenbart sich in der Inneneinrichtung. Treppen führen zu einzelnen, privaten, höhlenhaft anmutenden Kokons aus Fiberglas für zwei bis vier Personen. Diese Kokons verteilen sich im Restaurant über mehrere Ebenen.

Que le nom de ce bar à vins situé dans une cave soit ici le thème, cela se remarque dans l'architecture intérieure. Des escaliers mènent à de jolis cocons de fibres de verre individuels, privés, sorte de petites grottes pour deux à quatre personnes. Ces cocons sont disposés dans le restaurant sur plusieurs niveaux.

Que el nombre de la bodega alojada en un sótano constituye aquí el programa se manifiesta en la instalación interior. Las escaleras conducen a varios capullos, privados, que recuerdan a una cueva, hechos de fibra de vidrio, para dos hasta cuatro personas. Estos capullos están distribuidos en el restaurante por varios niveles.

Che il nome dell'enoteca ubicata nel piano interrato sia tutto un programma, lo rivela già l'arredamento. Delle scale conducono a singoli salottini privati disposti su più piani, nicchie in fibra di vetro dalle sembianze di piccole caverne che possono ospitare da due a quattro persone.

Hideo Horikawa Architect & Associates

3-12-1 Amanuma, Suginami-ku
Tokyo 167-0032
Japan

Photos by Martin Nicholas Kunz

Cocoon Mayu

Kamiyamacho 40-3, B1F
Tokyo 150-0042
Japan

J-Pop is a modern interpretation of Japanese pop culture and just as much art installation as restaurant. Strikingly bright colors and soft materials, reminiscent of foam, lend the room a retro and futuristic ambiance.

Das J-Pop ist eine moderne Interpretation der japanischen Pop-Kultur und ebenso Kunstinstallation wie Restaurant. Auffallend bunte Farben und weiche, an Schaumstoff erinnernde Materialien verleihen dem Raum ein retro-futuristisch wirkendes Ambiente.

Le J-Pop est une version moderne de la culture Pop japonaise et aussi bien une installation artistique qu'un restaurant. Des couleurs vives qui sautent aux yeux et des matériaux souples qui rappellent de la mousse confère à l'espace une ambiance rétro-futuriste.

El J-Pop es una interpretación moderna de la cultura pop japonesa y es tanto una instalación de arte como un restaurante. Los colores vivos llamativos y los materiales blandos, que recuerdan a la goma espuma, dotan al espacio de un ambiente que parece retro-futurista.

Con la sua duplice funzione di area di allestimento artistico e di ristorante, il locale J-Pop si presenta come un esempio di interpretazione moderna della cultura pop giapponese. Il contrasto creato dai colori vistosi e dai materiali morbidi simili alla gommapiuma conferisce all'ambiente un'atmosfera retrofuturistica.

Katsunori Suzuki, Fantastic Design Works Inc.

201 Maison Minami Aoyama
Tokyo 107-0062
Japan
www.f-fantastic.com

Photos by Martin Nicholas Kunz

J-Pop Shibuya

7F Shibuya-ku Beam, 31-2 Udagawa-cho
Tokyo 163-1055
Japan
www.j-popcafe.com/shibuya

Stools and tables in bright, candy colors are placed on a floor, tiled in a mosaic-style pattern, just like in a dream landscape. A computer-controlled system is responsible for the lighting and projects pictures and films onto the wall areas, so producing changing moods every day.

Wie in einer Traumlandschaft verteilen sich auf einem mosaikartig gefliesten Boden Hocker und Tische in bunten Bonbon-Farben. Ein computergesteuertes System ist für die Beleuchtung verantwortlich, projiziert Bilder und Filme auf Wandflächen und erzeugt so täglich wechselnde Stimmungen.

Comme dans un paysage de rêve, les tabourets et les tables aux couleurs bonbon sont disposés sur un sol carrelé comme une mosaïque. Un système contrôlé par ordinateur gère l'éclairage, projette des images et des films sur les murs et crée ainsi des ambiances chaque jour différentes.

Como en un paisaje de ensueño, los taburetes y las mesas de colores chillones se distribuyen sobre un suelo de baldosas a modo de mosaico. Un sistema dirigido por ordenador es responsable de la iluminación, proyecta imágenes y películas sobre superficies de la pared produciendo así ambientes que cambian a diario.

Come a punteggiare un paesaggio irreale, sgabelli e tavoli in vivaci colori confetto sono disposti su un pavimento piastrellato tipo mosaico. Un sistema computerizzato regola l'illuminazione e proietta immagini e film sulle pareti, dando vita a mutevoli atmosfere di giorno in giorno diverse.

Claudio Colucci Design

2-9-11, Nishi-azabu, Minato-ku
Tokyo 106-0031
Japan
www.colucci-design.com

Photos by Nacása & Partners Inc.
Martin Nicholas Kunz (p. 69)

Moph

15-1 Shibuya Parco Part 1, 1F Udagawatyo, Shibuya-ku
Tokyo 150-0042
Japan
www.moph.jp

In the Sentosa Resort & Spa, a unique location and architectural finesse unite high above the ocean. The restaurant was divided up with soft transitions into open and enclosed, sunny and shady areas. In this way and by using natural building substances, architecture and nature form an ideal synthesis.

Im The Sentosa Resort & Spa treffen hoch über dem Ozean einmalige Lage und architektonische Finesse aufeinander. Unter Verwendung natürlicher Baustoffe wurde das Restaurant mit sanften Übergängen in offene und geschlossene, sonnige und schattige Bereiche eingeteilt, sodass Architektur und Natur eine ideale Synthese eingehen.

On trouve au The Sentosa Resort & Spa la conjugaison d'une architecture raffinée et d'un site exceptionnel au-dessus de l'océan. Le restaurant est agencé en différents espaces, ouverts et fermés, ensoleillés et ombragés dont les passages de l'un à l'autre se font en douceur grâce à l'utilisation de matériaux naturels, ce qui crée une synthèse idéale entre architecture et nature.

En el The Sentosa Resort & Spa se unen a gran altura sobre el océano una situación excepcional y una finura arquitectónica. Empleando materiales de construcción naturales el restaurante fue dividido por pasos suaves en recintos abiertos y cerrados, al sol y a la sombra, de modo que la arquitectura y la naturaleza conciertan una síntesis ideal.

Nel The Sentosa Resort & Spa ben si sposano, l'ubicazione d'eccezione, sospesa sull'oceano, e la raffinatezza architettonica. L'uso di materiali esclusivamente naturali nonché la fluidità di spazi aperti e chiusi, solari e ombreggiati consentono all'architettura di raggiungere una sintesi ideale con la natura.

Yasuhiro Koichi Design Studio SPIN

JM Apartment 202, 3-26-45 Honcho Nkano-ku
Tokyo 164-0012
Japan

Photos by Martin Nicholas Kunz

Cliff

The Sentosa Resort & Spa
2 Bukit Manis Road
Singapore 099891
Singapore
www.beaufort.com.sg

La Scala in The Sukhothai Hotel is characterized by the blend of Italian cuisine and Thai tradition. The rooms are optimally used. A formal reduction of furnishing, restrained colors and glass walls make what is a narrow room for Asian standards appear spacious.

Die Verbindung von italienischer Küche und thailändischer Tradition kennzeichnet das La Scala im The Sukhothai Hotel. Die Räumlichkeiten sind optimal genutzt. Eine formale Reduktion der Einrichtung, gedeckte Farben und Glaswände lassen den, für asiatische Verhältnisse, beengten Raum großzügig erscheinen.

C'est l'association de la cuisine italienne et de la tradition thaïlandaise qui est la marque du restaurant La Scala à The Sukhothai Hotel. L'espace est utilisé au mieux. Une réduction des formes dans l'aménagement, des couleurs atténuées et des murs de verre donnent une ampleur à la pièce, qui est relativement étroite pour les conditions asiatiques.

La unión de la cocina italiana y la tradición tailandesa caracterizan La Scala en The Sukhothai Hotel. Las salas están aprovechadas de forma óptima. Una reducción formal de la decoración, los colores apagados y las paredes de vidrio hacen que el espacio, estrecho para las condiciones asiáticas, parezca amplio.

La combinazione di cucina italiana e tailandese costituisce l'elemento caratterizzante del ristorante La Scala a The Sukhothai Hotel. Gli spazi sono sfruttati in modo ottimale. Riduzione formale, colori spenti e vetrate a tutta parete fanno apparire più ampio lo spazio che, secondo gli standard asiatici, potrebbe sembrare piuttosto limitato.

Yasuhiro Koichi Design Studio SPIN

JM Apartment 202, 3-26-45 Honcho Nkano-ku
Tokyo 164-0012
Japan

Photos by Martin Nicholas Kunz

La Scala

The Sukhothai Hotel
13/3 South Sathorn Road
Bangkok
Thailand 10120
www.sukhothai.com

Architects & Designers

3deluxe

In 1992, communication designers Andreas and Stephan Lauhoff and interior architect Nikolaus Schweiger formed a partnership as 3deluxe in Wiesbaden. In the mid-1990s, the designer Dieter Brell joined them. Today, the interdisciplinary team includes 20 people from specialist areas of art, architecture, graphics, media and product design. On the basis of this far-reaching skills' pool, 3deluxe develops comprehensive design solutions, which project an integrated aesthetics from graphic imaging to media staging and architecture.

1992 schließen sich die Kommunikationsdesigner Andreas und Stephan Lauhoff sowie der Innenarchitekt Nikolaus Schweiger in Wiesbaden zu 3deluxe zusammen. Mitte der Neuzigerjahre stößt der Designer Dieter Brell hinzu. Heute umfasst das interdisziplinäre Team 20 Personen, die den Fachgebieten Kunst, Architektur, Grafik-, Medien- oder Produktdesign entstammen. Auf der Basis dieses weit reichenden Kompetenzspektrums entwickelt 3deluxe umfassende Designlösungen, die vom grafischen Erscheinungsbild über die mediale Inszenierung bis hin zur Architektur eine zusammenhängende Ästhetik ausstrahlen.

En 1992, les designers en communication Andreas et Stephan Lauhoff ainsi que l'architecte d'intérieur Nikolaus Schweiger s'associent pour former 3deluxe à Wiesbaden. Au milieu des années quatre-vingt-dix, le designer Dieter Brell se joint à eux. Aujourd'hui l'équipe interdisciplinaire est composée de 20 personnes qui viennent des domaines de l'art, de l'architecture, du graphisme, du design audiovisuel et du design industriel. Sur la base de ce très large spectre de compétences 3deluxe développe un design apportant des solutions très diverses qui, partant du graphisme, en passant par la mise en scène médiatique jusqu'à l'architecture expriment une esthétique cohérente.

En 1992 se unen en Wiesbaden como 3deluxe los diseñadores de comunicación Andreas y Stephan Lauhoff así como el arquitecto de interiores Nikolaus Schweiger. A mediados de los años noventa se añade a

ellos el diseñador Dieter Brell. Hoy el equipo interdisciplinario abarca a 20 personas que proceden de las especialidades del arte, la arquitectura, el diseño gráfico, de medios de comunicación o de productos. Sobre la base de este extenso espectro de competencias 3deluxe desarrolla amplias soluciones de diseño que irradian una estética coherente desde la apariencia gráfica pasando por la escenificación de los medios de comunicación hasta la arquitectura.

Lo studio 3deluxe nasce a Wiesbaden nel 1992 dal sodalizio fra i communication designer Andreas e Stephan Lauhoff e l'architetto d'interni Nikolaus Schweiger. Nella metà degli anni Novanta approda allo studio il designer Dieter Brell. Oggi il team interdisciplinare di 3deluxe è composto di 20 persone con diversi background che spaziano dal settore artistico ed architettonico fino ad arrivare al graphic design, al media design e al product design. L'ampio spettro di competenze dei collaboratori consente allo studio di offrire delle soluzioni di design a tutto tondo capaci di armonizzare le strategie grafiche, multimediali ed architettoniche a beneficio dell'estetica.

Acconci Studio

Born in New York in 1940, Vito Acconci made a name for himself with his free works as the enfant terrible of the art business. From 1980, he devoted himself to unfamiliar furnishing pieces, space design and projects at the intersection of architecture and sculpture. In 1989, he opened the Acconci Studio, an architectural and design workshop. In 2001, the Milwaukee Museum of Art showed a retrospective, including over two decades of creative work, about Acconci's designs and partially completed "Acts of Architecture".

1940 in New York geboren, wurde Vito Acconci mit seinen freien Arbeiten als Enfant terrible des Kunstbetriebs bekannt. Seit 1980 widmet er sich verfremdeten Einrichtungsgegenständen, Platzgestaltungen und

Projekten im Grenzbereich zwischen Architektur und Skulptur. 1989 eröffnete er das Acconci Studio, eine Architektur- und Designwerkstatt. Das Milwaukee Museum of Art zeigte 2001 eine über zwei Schaffensjahrzehnte umfassende Retrospektive zu den von Acconci konzipierten und zum Teil realisierten „Acts of Architecture".

Né en 1940 à New York Vito Acconci avec ses travaux très libres est devenu l'enfant terrible du milieu artistique. Depuis 1980, il travaille avec du mobilier qu'il détourne de son usage habituel et se consacre à l'aménagement de places et à des projets à la frontière entre l'architecture et la sculpture. En 1989, il a ouvert l'Acconci Studio, un atelier d'architecture et de design. Le Milwaukee Museum of Art a consacrée en 2001 une rétrospective montrant plus de deux décennies de création des « Acts of Architecture », qui ont été conçus et en partie réalisés par Acconci.

Nacido en Nueva York en 1940, Vito Acconci se hizo conocido con sus trabajos libres como el enfant terrible de la empresa del arte. Desde 1980 se dedica a objetos de decoración distanciados, a configuraciones del espacio y proyectos en la frontera entre la arquitectura y la escultura. En 1989 abrió el Acconci Studio, un taller de arquitectura y diseño. El Milwaukee Museum of Art mostró en 2001 una retrospectiva de los "Acts of Architecture" concebidos y en parte realizados por Acconci y que abarcó más de dos decenios de su creación.

Nato a New York nel 1940, Vito Acconci si è affermato nel panorama artistico con i suoi lavori indipendenti che gli hanno valso la fama di enfant terribile. A partire dal 1980 si dedica all'estraniamento di oggetti d'arredamento, a realizzazioni d'interventi in spazi pubblici e a progettazioni al limite fra architettura e scultura. Nel 1989 fonda l'Acconci Studio, un laboratorio di architettura e design. Nel 2001 al Milwaukee Museum of Art viene esposta una retrospettiva dedicata a più di due decenni creativi dell'artista sugli "Acts of Architecture" concepiti e in parte realizzati da Acconci.

Arquitectonica

Arquitectonica was founded in 1977 as an experimental studio in Coral Gables. Of the five founding members, Laurinda Spear and Fernando Fort-Brescia have gained a reputation as leading designers. Arquitectonica is meanwhile a respected architectural firm and supervises projects worldwide with 250 employees. As well as their headquarters in Miami, they have offices in Los Angeles, Paris, Manila, Lima, Buenos Aires, São Paulo, Hong Kong and Shanghai. Their clear, geometrical architectural language is influenced by Russian Constructivism and gains a playful lightness with a postmodern splash of color.

1977 wurde Arquitectonica als experimentelles Studio in Coral Gables gegründet. Von den fünf Gründern haben sich Laurinda Spear und Fernando Fort-Brescia als bestimmende Designer profiliert. Inzwischen ist Arquitectonica ein angesehenes Architekturbüro und betreut mit 250 Mitarbeitern weltweite Projekte. Neben ihrer Zentrale in Miami sind sie mit Büros in Los Angeles, Paris, Manila, Lima, Buenos Aires, São Paulo, Hongkong und Shanghai vertreten. Ihre klare geometrische, vom russischen Konstruktivismus geprägte Architektursprache erfährt durch eine postmoderne Farbenpracht eine spielerische Leichtigkeit.

C'est en tant que studio expérimental qu'est créé Arquitectonica en 1977 à Coral Gables. Parmi les cinq fondateurs, Laurinda Spear et Fernando Fort-Brescia se sont imposés en tant que designers reconnus. Entre temps Arquitectonica est devenu un bureau d'architecture renommé et il emploie 250 collaborateurs pour des projets internationaux. Outre leur siège à Miami, ils ont des bureaux à Los Angeles, Paris, Manille, Lima, Buenos Aires, Sao Paulo, Hongkong et Shanghai. La splendeur postmoderne des couleurs confère à leur langage architectural, d'une géométrie claire inspirée du constructivisme russe, une légèreté ludique.

Arquitectonica fue fundada en 1977 como un estudio experimental en Coral Gables. De los cinco cofundadores, Laurinda Spear y Fernando Fort-Brescia se han distinguido como los diseñadores determinantes. Entretanto, Arquitectonica es una oficina de arquitectura apreciada y, con 250 empleados, lleva proyectos en todo el mundo. Junto a su central en Miami están representados con oficinas en Los Angeles, Paris, Manila, Lima, Buenos Aires, São Paulo, Hongkong y Shanghai. Su claro lenguaje arquitectónico geométrico, marcado por el constructivismo ruso, experimenta una ligereza juguetona por medio de una riqueza de colores postmoderna.

Arquitectonica è nato come laboratorio sperimentale di architettura a Coral Gables nel 1977. Per la loro spiccata personalità di designer, Laurinda Spear e Fernando Fort-Brescia sono andati assumendo un ruolo guida nel team dei cinque soci fondatori. Oggi Arquitectonica è un prestigioso studio di architettura che conta 250 collaboratori ed opera su scala mondiale. Alla sede centrale di Miami si sono via affiancati altri studi aperti a Los Angeles, Parigi, Manila, Lima, Buenos Aires, São Paulo, Hong Kong e Shanghai. Il tripudio di colori di matrice postmoderna conferisce al chiaro linguaggio geometrico formatosi alla scuola del costruttivismo russo una leggerezza ludica.

Bender Design

Volker Bender Design mainly plans and sets up trade fair stands, presentation rooms, buildings for Formula 1 VIP areas and roadshows for companies like BMW. Reduction and high-tech minimalism are dominant principles for the selection of materials and work on detail. Projects are completed exactly to plan, thanks to the company's own production workshop for steel, colored metals, glass and wood, which make it possible to appreciate the company's experience in terms of quality irrespective of the size of the project.

Volker Bender Design plant und realisiert überwiegend Messestände, Präsentationsräume, Gebäude für den Formel-1-VIP-Bereich und Roadshows für Unternehmen wie BMW. In der Wahl der Materialien und der Detailbearbeitung sind Reduktion und High-tech-Minimalismus die beherrschenden Prinzipien. Mittels einer eigenen Produktionsstätte für Stahl, Buntmetalle, Glas und Holz werden zielgenaue Umsetzungen erreicht, die unabhängig von der Größe des Projekts, die Erfahrung des Unternehmens qualitativ erlebbar macht.

Volker Bender Design conçoit et réalise surtout des stands pour les foires, des espaces de présentation, des bâtiments pour les espaces VIP de Formule 1 et des « roadshows » pour des entreprises comme BMW. Dans le choix des matériaux et dans le travail des détails, la sobriété et le minimalisme high tech sont les principes dominants. Grâce à un propre site de production pour acier, métaux lourds non ferreux, verre et bois, les matériaux peuvent être transformés exacte-

ment en fonction des objectifs. Cela confère, indépendamment des grands projets, une expérience à l'entreprise dont on ne peut que constater la qualité de son travail.

Volker Bender Design proyecta y realiza principalmente estands de ferias, salas de presentación, edificios para el recinto VIP de fórmula 1 y roadshows para empresas como BMW. Los principios dominantes en la elección de los materiales y el tratamiento de los detalles son la reducción y el minimalismo de alta tecnología. Por medio de un lugar de producción propio para el acero, los metales de colores, el vidrio y la madera se consiguen unas realizaciones precisas haciendo que la experiencia de la empresa pueda experimentarse cualitativamente con independencia del tamaño del proyecto.

Lo studio Volker Bender Design è specializzato nella progettazione e realizzazione di allestimenti fieristici, sale presentazioni, ampi spazi ricettivi per i protagonisti VIP della Formula 1 e roadshows per aziende come la BMW. I principi ispiratori tanto nella scelta dei materiali quanto nell'elaborazione del dettaglio sono la riduzione ed il minimalismo high-tech. Grazie ad un proprio laboratorio di produzione per l'acciaio, i metalli non ferrosi, il vetro e il legno sono possibili realizzazioni accuratissime che indipendentemente dalle dimensioni del progetto danno prova della grande esperienza maturata dall'azienda.

Boesel Benkert Hohberg Architekten

In 2002, the three Munich architects teamed up to form an office community. Andreas Boesel, born in 1953, studied computer science and architecture at Munich's Technical University. Jörg Hohberg, born in 1965, and Gunter Benkert, born in 1967, also studied architecture in Munich at the Technical University. Within two years, they earned a reputation as leading designers for top architectures, institutes and administrative projects as well as apartments and restaurants.

2002 schlossen sich die drei Architekten in München zu einer Bürogemeinschaft zusammen. Andreas Boesel, geb. 1953, studierte an der TU München Informatik und Architektur. Jörg Hohberg, geb. 1965, und Gunter Benkert, geb. 1967, studierten ebenfalls an der TU in München Architektur. Innerhalb von zwei Jahren haben sie sich als bestimmende

Gestalter für anspruchsvolle Architekturen für Instituts- und Verwaltungsbauten, Wohnbauten und die Gastronomie profiliert.

En 2002 les trois architectes s'associent pour former un bureau à Munich. Andreas Boesel, né en 1963, a étudié à l'université technique de Munich l'informatique et l'architecture. Jörg Hohberg, né en 1965, et Gunter Benkert, né en 1967, ont étudié aussi l'architecture à l'université technique de Munich. En deux ans ils se sont affirmés en tant que concepteurs reconnus dans le domaine de l'architecture de haut niveau pour des constructions d'instituts et bâtiments d'administration ainsi que des ensembles d'habitations et de restaurants.

En 2002 se unieron los tres arquitectos en una comunidad de oficinas en Munich. Andreas Boesel, nacido en 1953, estudió informática y arquitectura en la TU de Munich. Jörg Hohberg, nacido en 1965, y Gunter Benkert, nacido en 1967, estudiaron igualmente arquitectura en la TU de Munich. En el transcurso de dos años se han distinguido como diseñadores determinantes por sus arquitecturas exigentes tanto para edificios administrativos y de institutos como para edificios de viviendas y gastronomía.

Nel 2002 i tre architetti hanno deciso di unire le loro competenze e di fondare assieme uno studio a Monaco. Nato nel 1953, Andreas Boesel ha studiato informatica e architettura all'Università Tecnica (TU) di Monaco. Jörg Hohberg (nato nel 1965) e Gunter Benkert (nato nel 1967) hanno studiato architettura presso la stessa università. A due anni dalla creazione dell'omonimo studio, i tre architetti si sono saputi imporre all'attenzione per le progettazioni architettoniche ambiziose di istituti pubblici ed edifici amministrativi nonché per le loro realizzazioni nel campo dell'edilizia residenziale e della gastronomia.

Fabio Maria Ceccarelli

The Florentine architect Fabio Maria Ceccarelli has a wide range of experience in the fields of planning, architecture, interior architecture and product design and has specialized in hotel and restaurants. His studio has desgined several rooms of the most diverse kind in the restaurants Uliassi, Madonnina del pescatore, the Saltatappo wine bar, the Anikò and Anikò suscibar as well as the Officina. In the process, it has created original, contemporary designs, which are functional and also involve the culture of local cuisine and the respective location.

Der Florentiner Architekt Fabio Maria Ceccarelli hat breit gefächerte Erfahrungen in den Bereichen Planung, Architektur, Innenarchitektur und Produktdesign und hat sich auf den Hotel- und Restaurantbereich spezialisiert. Sein Büro hat mit den Restaurants Uliassi, Madonnina del pescatore, der Weinbar Saltatappo, dem Anikò und Anikò suscibar sowie dem Officina mehrere Räumlichkeiten verschiedenster Art gestaltet und dabei originelle zeitgenössische Designs schaffen, die funktional sind und zugleich die lokale Küchenkultur und den jeweiligen Ort mit einbeziehen.

L'architecte florentin Fabio Maria Ceccarelli a acquis de larges expériences dans le domaine de la planification, de l'architecture, de l'architecture intérieure et du design de produits et il s'est spécialisé dans le secteur de l'hôtellerie et de la restauration. Avec les restaurants Uliassi, Madonnina del pescatore, le bar à vins Saltatappo, Anikò et Anikò suscibar ainsi qu'avec Officina, son bureau a conçu plusieurs espaces de types différents et a ainsi créé des designs contemporains originaux, qui sont fonctionnels et qui en même temps prennent en compte chaque lieu et sa culture culinaire.

El arquitecto florentino Fabio Maria Ceccarelli tiene una experiencia muy variada en los terrenos de la planificación, arquitectura, arquitectura de interiores y el diseño de productos y se ha especializado en el ámbito de hoteles y restaurantes. Su oficina ha diseñado con los restaurantes Uliassi, Madonnina del pescatore, la vinatería Saltatappo, el Anikò y el Anikò suscibar así como el Officina varios espacios del tipo más distinto creando con ellos originales diseños contemporáneos que son funcionales y, al mismo tiempo, incluyen la cultura culinaria local y el lugar respectivo.

L'architetto fiorentino Fabio Maria Ceccarelli ha maturato svariate esperienze nei settori progettazione, architettura, architettura d'interni e product design prima di specializzarsi nell'ambito nel campo del design alberghiero e del dining design. Con i ristoranti Uliassi, Madonnina del pescatore, l'enoteca Saltatappo, l'Anikò e l'Anikò suscibar nonché con l'Officina il suo studio ha creato un ampio spettro di interior design rivelando soluzioni originali di design contemporaneo che non sacrificano alla funzionalità la cultura gastronomica locale e il suo legame con il territorio.

Michael Chow Design Group

A native of Shanghai, Michael Chow, who is amongst other things a designer, painter and actor all in one, graduated in architecture in London. Afterwards, he worked as a painter and sculptor. In 1965, he designed boutiques for, among others, Giorgio Armani. In 1968, Michael Chow made a name for himself by putting into action his strictly minimalist concept for the first time in his London restaurant, MR CHOW. This was one of Europe's very first design restaurants and the first in a series of restaurants under this name, which were all personally designed by Chow. His works make the architect, who lives in Los Angeles since 1985, into a sought after designer for unusual locations.

Der in Shanghai geborene Michael Chow, u. a. Designer, Maler und Schauspieler in Personalunion, absolvierte sein Architekturstudium in London. Anschließend war er als Maler und Bildhauer tätig. Seit 1965 gestaltete er Boutiquen u. a. für Giorgio Armani. 1968 machte Michael Chow von sich reden, als er in London erstmalig sein streng minimalistisches Konzept im Restaurant MR CHOW umsetzte, einem der ersten Designrestaurants in Europa überhaupt und das erste einer Reihe von Restaurants dieses Namens, die er alle persönlich entwarf. Seine Arbeiten machen den seit 1985 in Los Angeles lebenden Architekten zum gefragten Designer außergewöhnlicher Locations.

Michael Chow qui est né à Shanghai et qui est à la fois entre autres designer, peintre et comédien, a étudié l'architecture à Londres. Il a ensuite travaillé comme peintre et sculpteur. Depuis 1965, il conçoit des boutiques, entre autres pour Giorgio Armani. En 1968 il fait parler de lui lorsqu'il transpose pour la première fois son concept rigoureusement minimaliste en réalisant le restaurant MR CHOW à Londres, un des premiers restaurants de designers en Europe et le premier d'une ligne de restaurants de ce nom, qu'il a personnellement conçu.

Michael Chow, nacido en Shanghai, entre otras cosas diseñador, pintor y actor mediante unión personal, estudió su carrera de arquitectura en Londres. Después de ello, trabajó como pintor y escultor. Desde 1965 diseña boutiques, entre otros, para Giorgio Armani. En 1968 Michael Chow hizo que se hablara de él cuando realizó por primera vez su plan estrictamente minimalista en el restaurante MR CHOW, uno de los primeros restaurantes de diseño en Europa en general y el primero de una serie de restaurantes con este nombre, todos ellos proyectados personalmente por él. Sus trabajos hacen del arquitecto, que reside en Los Ángeles desde 1985, un solicitado diseñador de emplazamientos excepcionales.

Nato a Shanghai, Michael Chow è una personalità eclettica, capace di essere contemporaneamente designer, pittore ed attore e molto altro. Dopo aver concluso i suoi studi di architettura a Londra, ha lavorato come pittore e scultore. Dal 1965 svolge un'attività come shop designer, ad esempio delle boutique Giorgio Armani. Nel 1968 Michael Chow è tornato a far parlare di sé per la realizzazione a Londra del ristorante MR CHOW ispirato ad uno stile rigorosamente minimalista decisamente nuovo. Si trattava infatti del primo ristorante design in Europa nonché del primo dei ristoranti Mr Chow, una catena di locali progettati personalmente dall'architetto che dal 1985 vive a Los Angeles. Le sue opere gli hanno valso la fama di richiesto designer di locations d'eccezione.

Claudio Colucci Design

Claudio Colucci was born in 1965 in Locarno, Switzerland. In 1992, he completed his studies in Geneva and Paris with a degree in interior architecture. He then moved to

London to work for Ron Arad and Nigel Coates, Pascal Mourgue in Paris, as well as for Thompson Multimedia under the direction of Philippe Starck. In 1994, he founded RADI Designers with four other colleagues, since 1996 he has worked for IDÈE Design. In 2000, Claudio Colucci began a freelance career and lives and works mainly in Paris and Tokyo. His main focus is on exhibition design, interior architecture as well as product design and scenery.

Claudio Colucci wurde 1965 in Locarno/ Schweiz geboren. Seine Studien in Genf und Paris beendete er 1992 mit einem Abschluss als Innenarchitekt. Anschließend arbeitete er bei Ron Arad und Nigel Coates in London, Pascal Mourgue in Paris sowie für Thompson Multimedia unter der Leitung von Philippe Starck. 1994 gründete er mit vier weiteren Designern RADI Designers, seit 1996 arbeitete er für IDÈE Design. 2000 machte sich Claudio Colucci selbstständig und lebt und arbeitet vorwiegend in Paris und Tokio. Sein Tätigkeitsschwerpunkt liegt in der Ausstellungskonzeption, der Innenarchitektur sowie in den Bereichen Produktdesign und Szenenbild.

Claudio Colucci est né en 1965 à Locarno en Suisse. Il fait ses études à Genève et Paris et obtient en 1992 son diplôme en architecture intérieure. Il travaille ensuite chez Ron Aras et Nigel Coates à Londres, Pascal Mourgue à Paris ainsi que pour Thompson Multimedia sous la direction de Philippe Starck. En 1994, il crée avec quatre autres designers RADI Designers, depuis 1996 il travaille pour IDÈE Design. En 2000 Claudio Colucci fonde son propre bureau, il vit et travaille la plupart du temps à Paris et Tokyo. Les points forts de son travail sont la conception d'expositions, l'architecture intérieure ainsi que les secteurs du design de produits et de scénographie.

Claudio Colucci nació en 1965 en Locarno (Suiza). Sus estudios los concluyó en Ginebra y París en 1992 con un título de arquitectura de interiores. A continuación trabajó para Ron Arad y Nigel Coates en Londres, para Pascal Mourgue en París, así como para Thompson Multimedia bajo la dirección de Philippe Starck. En 1994 fundó RADI Designers, a partir de 1996 trabajó para IDÈE Design. En 2000 Claudio Colucci se independizó y vive y trabaja principalmente en París y Tokio. Los puntos centrales de su trabajo son la concepción de exposiciones, la arquitectura de interiores así como los ámbitos del diseño de productos y la escenografía.

Claudio Colucci è nato a Locarno/Svizzera nel 1965. Il percorso formativo compiuto a Ginevra e Parigi si è concluso con la laurea in architettura d'interni. In seguito ha iniziato la sua attività lavorativa presso gli studi Ron Arad e Nigel Coates a Londra, Pascal Mourgue a Parigi nonché per Thompson Multimedia sotto la guida di Philippe Starck. Nel 1994 ha dato vita, insieme ad altri 4 designer, a RADI Designers. A partire dal 1996 ha lavorato per IDÈE Design. Nel 2000 Claudio Colucci decide di mettersi in proprio: da allora vive e lavora prevalentemente a Parigi e Tokio. Le esperienze maturate lo hanno portato a specializzarsi nella concezione di esposizioni, nell'architettura d'interni nonché nel product design e nella realizzazione di scenografie.

concrete architectural associates

concrete architectural associates was established in 1999 by Gilian Schrofer, Rob Wagemans and Eric van Dillen. The Dutch architects work intuitively by pooling their ideas. For them, architecture is a poetic discipline and therefore an expression of man's wishes and dreams. Art or design are for concrete not applications on buildings, but for pictures, rituals, light moods, color values, an integral part of the whole. They have attracted international awareness with their designs for shops, hotels and restaurants.

concrete architectural associates wurde 1999 von Gilian Schrofer, Rob Wagemans und Eric van Dillen gegründet. Intuitiv bewegen sich die niederländischen Architekten in dem Pool ihrer Ideen. Für sie ist Architektur eine poetische Disziplin und somit Ausdruck von Wünschen und Träumen der Menschen. Kunst oder Design sind für concrete keine Applikationen an Gebäuden, sondern Bilder, Rituale, Lichtstimmungen, Farbwerte, organischer Teil des Ganzen. Mit ihren Entwürfen für Läden, Hotels und Restaurants haben sie weltweit Aufsehen erregt.

concrete architectural associates a été fondé en 1999 par Gilian Schrofer, Rob Wagemans et Eric van Dillen. Les architectes néerlandais se meuvent avec beaucoup d'intuition dans le bain de leurs idées. Pour eux l'architecture est une discipline poétique qui est l'expression des désirs et des rêves des hommes. Pour concrete, l'art ou le design ne sont pas des éléments que l'on applique simplement aux bâtiments, mais les images, rituels, ambiances de lumière, valeurs chromatiques font partie de l'ensemble pour former une unité. Ils ont fait sensation dans le monde entier avec leurs projets de magasins, d'hôtels et restaurants.

concrete architectural associates fue fundada en 1999 por Gilian Schrofer, Rob Wagemans y Eric van Dillen. Los arquitectos holandeses se mueven de forma intuitiva dentro del pool de sus ideas. Para ellos la arquitectua es una disciplina poética y, con ello, la expresión de los deseos y sueños del ser humano. El arte o el diseño no son para concrete unas aplicaciones en edificios sino imágenes, rituales, ambientes de luz, valores de color, una parte orgánica del todo. Con sus proyectos para tiendas, hoteles y restaurantes han causado sensación mundial.

Lo studio concrete architectural associates è stato fondato nel 1999 da Gilian Schrofer, Rob Wagemans ed Eric van Dillen. Gli architetti nederlandesi attingono istintivamente dal loro pool di idee. Secondo la loro concezione, l'architettura è disciplina poetica e come tale espressione dei desideri e dei sogni dell'uomo: l'arte e il design non sono realizzazioni concrete bensì immagini, rituali, atmosfere di luce, valori cromatici, parte organica del tutto. Le loro progettazioni di negozi, hotel e ristoranti hanno suscitato scalpore in tutto il mondo.

Conran & Parnters

Terence Conran, born in 1931, is an active designer, restaurateur and publicist. In 1956, he founded the Conran Design Group with subsidiaries in London, Paris and Hong Kong. Conran Shops in London, Paris and Tokyo offer modern design and furnishing pieces. In 1964, he started the firm Habitat and in 1980 Conran & Partners. The agency's main focus is in the areas of architecture, urban planning, communication and interior design. His projects are constantly setting standards, such as his restaurants in London, New York and Paris, whose interior design establishes new trends.

Terence Conran, geb. 1931, ist als Designer, Gastronom und Publizist aktiv. 1956 gründete er die Conran Design Group mit Niederlassungen in London, Paris und Hongkong. Conran Shops in London, Paris und Tokio bieten modernes Design und Einrichtungsgegenstände an. 1964 gründete er die Firma Habitat und 1980 Conran & Partners. Der Schwerpunkt der Agentur liegt in den Bereichen Architektur, Stadtgestaltung, Kommunikations- und Interieur-Design. Seine Projekte setzen immer wieder Maßstäbe, wie beispielsweise seine Restaurants in London, New York und Paris, die in ihrer Innengestaltung stilbildend wirken.

Terence Conran, né en 1931, a des activités en tant que designer, restaurateur et publiciste. En 1956 il a fondé le Conran Design Group avec des filiales à Londres, Paris et Hongkong. Les Conran shops de Londres, Paris et Tokyo proposent un design moderne et du mobilier. En 1964 il a créé la firme Habitat et en 1980 Conran & Partners. Les principaux secteurs de prédilection de l'agence sont les domaines de l'architecture, de l'urbanisme, le design de communication et le design d'intérieur. Ses projets sont toujours des références, comme par exemple ses restaurants à Londres, New York et Paris, dont l'aménagement intérieur porte la marque du style bien particulier qu'elle a créé.

Terence Conran, nacido en 1931, trabaja como diseñador, gastrónomo y publicista. En 1956 fundó el Conran Design Group con filiales en Londres, París y Hongkong. Las tiendas de Conran en Londres, París y Tokio ofrecen un diseño moderno y objetos de decoración. En 1964 fundó la empresa Habitat y en 1980 Conran & Partners. El tema central de la agencia lo constituyen los ámbitos de la arquitectura, el diseño urbano y el diseño de comunicaciones e interiores. Sus proyectos marcan pautas una y otra vez, como por ejemplo sus restaurantes en Londres, Nueva York y París que producen un efecto creador de estilo en su diseño interior.

Terence Conran, nato nel 1931, lavora come designer, gastronomo e pubblicista. La creazione dello studio Conran Design Group con sedi a Londra, Parigi e Hong Kong risale al 1956. I negozi Conran a Londra, Parigi e Tokio offrono proposte di design moderno e soluzioni d'arredamento. Nel 1964 segue la creazione del marchio Habitat e nel 1980 della Conran & Partners. La progettazione architettonica, urbanistica, il communication design e l'interior design rappresentano i settori in cui il gruppo è andato via specializzandosi. Le realizzazioni firmate Conran creano tendenze sempre nuove, come ad esempio i suoi ristoranti a Londra, New York e Parigi che hanno dato vita ad uno stile tutto personale di interior design.

Corvino+Multari
Architetti Associati

Vincenzo Corvino, born in 1965, and Giovanni Multari, born in 1963, studied architecture in Naples. In 1995, they started their own architectural studio there, after Multari previously worked for Interpaln Architetti Associate in Naples. In 2000 and 2003, they won the "Cosenza Prize" for their projects and the "Centocittà Award" for architecture and interior architecture in 2001. Their style-setting designs have an objective impact without lacking feeling and they appear technical without being conventional. According to their own philosophy, their design has exactly to match aesthetics with functionality, in order to achieve the highest level of perfection.

Vincenzo Corvino, geb. 1965, und Giovanni Multari, geb. 1963, studierten Architektur in Neapel und gründeten 1995 daselbst ihr gemeinsames Architekturbüro, nachdem Multari zuvor bei Interpaln Architetti Associate in Neapel tätig war. Mit ihren Projekten gewannen sie 2000 und 2003 den „Cosenza Prize" und 2001 den „Centocittà Award" für Architektur und Innenarchitektur. Ihre stilbildenden Architekturen wirken sachlich ohne gefühllos zu sein und technisch ohne konventionell zu erscheinen. Gemäß ihrer Philosophie muss ihr Design Ästhetik und Funktionalität perfekt verbinden, um größtmögliche Vollkommenheit zu erreichen.

Vincenzo Corvino, né en 1965, et Giovanni Multari, né en 1963, ont étudié l'architecture à Naples et c'est là qu'ils ont ouvert ensemble un bureau d'architecture, après que Giovanni Multari ait travaillé au préalable chez Interpaln Architetti Associate à Naples. Ils ont reçu pour leurs projets, en 2000 et 2003 le prix « Cosenza Prize » et en 2001 le « Centocittà Award » pour l'architecture et l'architecture intérieure. Leurs architectures d'un style nouveau bien particulier sont sobres sans être froides et techniques sans paraître conventionnelles. Selon leur philo-

sophie, leur design doit conjuguer au mieux l'esthétique et la fonctionnalité afin d'obtenir la plus grande perfection possible.

Vincenzo Corvino, nacido en 1965, y Giovanni Multari, nacido en 1963, estudiaron arquitectura en Nápoles y fundaron allí mismo en 1995 su oficina conjunta de arquitectura después de que Multari hubiese trabajado en Nápoles en Interpaln Architetti Associate. Con sus proyectos ganaron en 2000 y 2003 el "Cosenza Prize" y en 2001 el "Centocittà Award" para arquitectura y arquitectura de interiores. Sus arquitecturas, que marcan un estilo, producen un efecto racional sin ser insensible y técnico sin parecer convencional. De acuerdo con su filosofía su diseño debe unir perfectamente la estética y la funcionalidad para alcanzar la mayor perfección posible.

Vincenzo Corvino, nato nel 1965, e Giovanni Multari, nato nel 1963, hanno studiato architettura a Napoli dove, nel 1995, hanno fondato insieme uno studio d'architettura nato in parte dall'esperienza maturata da Multari presso lo studio Interpaln Architetti Associate di Napoli. Per le loro realizzazioni hanno già vinto numerosi premi e riconoscimenti: nel 2000 e nel 2003 il "Cosenza Prize", nel 2001 il riconoscimento "Centocittà Award" per l'architettura e l'architettura d'interni. Le loro progettazioni architettoniche, espressione di uno stile tutto individuale, sono di impatto solido senza risultare fredde, tecnico senza sembrare convenzionali. Il principio ispirato dalla loro filosofia di fondo è che il design debba coniugare perfettamente estetica e funzionalità per potersi avvicinare il più possibile alla perfezione.

Dietrich | Untertrifaller
Architekten

Dietrich | Untertrifaller Architects has been going since 1994 and emerged from a partnership between Helmut Dietrich and Much Untertrifaller that began in 1986. Both architects were educated at the Technical University in Vienna. 15 employees usually work in offices in Bregenz and Vienna. The architects mainly work in Switzerland, Austria, Liechtenstein and Germany. In addition to office buildings and similar public and cultural offices, their main area of work is building apartments, interior architecture, furniture design as well as the design of exhibitions and museums.

Dietrich | Untertrifaller Architekten besteht seit 1994 und ging aus der 1986 begonnenen Zusammenarbeit zwischen Helmut Dietrich und Much Untertrifaller hervor, die beide an der TU Wien ausgebildet wurden. In den Büros in Bregenz und Wien sind in der Regel 15 Mitarbeiter beschäftigt. Die Architekten sind vor allem in der Schweiz, Österreich, Liechtenstein und Deutschland tätig. Neben Bürobauten und solchen des öffentlichen und kulturellen Lebens bilden der Wohnungsbau, die Innenarchitektur, das Möbeldesign sowie die Gestaltung von Ausstellungen und Museen weitere Arbeitsschwerpunkte.

Dietrich | Untertrifaller Architekten existe depuis 1994 et est né de la coopération initiée en 1986 entre Helmut Dietrich et Much Untertrifaller, qui ont été tous les deux formés à l'université technique de Vienne. 15 collaborateurs sont employés en temps normal dans les bureaux de Bregenz et Vienne. Les architectes travaillent surtout en Suisse, en Autriche, au Liechtenstein et en Allemagne. A côté d'immeubles de bureaux ou de bâtiments publics ou culturels, leurs points forts sont aussi les immeubles d'habitations, l'architecture intérieure, le design de meubles ainsi que la conception d'expositions et de musées.

Dietrich | Untertrifaller Architekten existe desde 1994 y resultó de la colaboración que Helmut Dietrich y Much Untertrifaller, ambos formados en la TU de Viena, iniciaron en 1986. En las oficinas de Bregenz y Viena trabajan normalmente 15 empleados. Los arquitectos son activos sobre todo en Suiza, Austria, Liechtenstein y Alemania. Otros puntos centrales de trabajo, junto a los edificios de oficinas y aquellos de la vida pública y cultural, lo conforman la construcción de viviendas, la arquitectura de interiores, el diseño de muebles así como la configuración de exposiciones y museos.

Dietrich | Untertrifaller Architekten nasce nel 1994 dalla collaborazione iniziata già nel 1986 fra Helmut Dietrich e Much Untertrifaller, entrambi formatisi alla Università Tecnica (TU) di Vienna. Negli studi con sede a Bregenz e Vienna lavora un team di circa 15 collaboratori. Gli architetti operano soprattutto in Svizzera, Austria, nel Liechtenstein e in Germania. Oltre all'edilizia per uffici e alle progettazioni di rilievo nell'ambito della vita pubblica e culturale, lo studio è andato

specializzandosi nell'edilizia residenziale, nell'architettura d'interni, nel design di mobili nonché nell'allestimento espositivo e museale.

Vincent van Duysen Architects

Vincent van Duysen finished his architectural studies in 1985 in Gent. Afterwards, he worked for several Belgian firms and as an assistant to Aldo Cibic in Milan, before he established his own firm in 1990. Works by Vincent van Duysen Architects are a blend of simplicity and sensuality with a preference for original forms and compact volumes. The company itself describes them as clear, elementary, minimalist and calm. Their successful works extend from furniture design to interior designs for houses, apartments, shops and commerical space as well as family homes.

Vincent van Duysen beendete sein Architekturstudium 1985 in Gent. Anschließend war er bei verschiedenen Büros in Belgien und als Assistent bei Aldo Cibic in Mailand tätig, bevor er 1990 sein eigenes Büros eröffnete. Die Arbeiten von Vincent van Duysen Architects sind eine Mischung aus Schlichtheit und Sinnlichkeit mit Vorliebe für ursprüngliche Formen und kompakte Volumen. Das Büro selbst bezeichnet sie als klar, elementar, minimalistisch und ruhig. Ihre erfolgreichen Arbeiten reichen von Möbeldesign über Innenraumgestaltungen für Häuser, Apartments, Läden und Geschäftsräume bis zu Einfamilienhäusern.

Vincent van Duysen a terminé ses études d'architecture à Gand en 1985. Il a travaillé ensuite dans plusieurs bureaux en Belgique, puis a été assistant chez Aldo Cibic à Milan, avant d'ouvrir son propre bureau en 1990. Les travaux de Vincent van Duysen représentent un mélange de sobriété et de sensualité avec une préférence pour les formes originelles et les volumes compacts. Le bureau décrit lui-même ses travaux comme étant clairs, élémentaires, minimalistes et sereins. Ses travaux qui ont beaucoup de succès vont du design de meubles à la réalisation de maisons individuelles en passant par l'aménagement d'intérieurs pour des maisons, des appartements, des magasins et locaux commerciaux.

Vincent van Duysen terminó su carrera de arquitectura en Gante en 1985. Después de ello trabajó en diferentes oficinas de Bélgica y como asistente para Aldo Cibic en Milán antes de abrir su propia oficina en 1990. Los trabajos de los Vincent van Duysen Architects son una mezcla de sencillez y sensualidad con una preferencia por las formas originales y los volúmenes compactos. La oficina misma los describe como claros, elementales, minimalistas y tranquilos. Sus trabajos llenos de éxito van desde el diseño de muebles pasando por los diseños de interiores hasta las casas, apartamentos, tiendas y locales de negocios hasta las casas unifamiliares.

Vincent van Duysen ha completato gli studi di architettura nel 1985 a Gent. In seguito ha iniziato la sua attività lavorativa presso diversi studi in Belgio e presso lo studio Aldo Cibic a Milano, dove ha lavorato in qualità di assistente, prima di fondare uno studio proprio nel 1990. I lavori dello studio Vincent van Duysen Architects nascono dalla combinazione di semplicità e sensualità con una chiara preferenza per le forme originarie e i volumi compatti. Lo studio definisce il proprio stile come pulito, essenziale, minimalista e privo di elementi irrequieti. Le realizzazioni di successo spaziano dal design di mobili e dall'interior design per spazi abitativi (case ed appartamenti), allo shop e office design fino ad arrivare alla progettazione di ville.

Escher Gune-Wardena Architecture

The Swiss national, Frank Escher, studied architecture at ETH (Swiss Technical College) in Zurich and Ravi Gune Wardena from Sri Lanka studied in Pomona/USA and Florence. In 1995, they both formed a partnership. Their range of work extends from apartment construction to commercial buildings and public projects in the USA and Canada. In 2003, they were accepted into the National Design Triennal and work as advisors to the Los Angeles Forum for Architecture and Urban Design. The architects have developed ideas and

projects together with artists in the field of contemporary art. Their work has been distinguished worldwide.

Der Schweizer Frank Escher studierte Architektur an der ETH in Zürich, Ravi Gune Wardena aus Sri Lanka in Pomona/USA und Florenz. 1995 schlossen sich beide zu einem Büro zusammen. Ihr Arbeitsspektrum reicht vom Wohnbau über Geschäftsgebäude bis zu öffentlichen Projekten in den USA und Kanada. 2003 wurden sie in das National Design Triennal aufgenommen und sind als Berater des Los Angeles Forum for Architecture and Urban Design tätig. Im Bereich der zeitgenössischen Kunst haben die Architekten Ideen und Projekte in Zusammenarbeit mit Künstlern entwickelt. Ihre Arbeiten sind weltweit ausgezeichnet worden.

Le Suisse Frank Escher a étudié l'architecture à l'ETH (Ecole Technique) de Zurich, Ravi Gune Wardena qui vient du Sri Lanka a étudié à Pomona/USA et à Florence. En 1995 ils fondent ensemble un bureau. Leur champ d'action va de la construction d'habitations jusqu'à des projets publics aux Etats-Unis et au Canada, en passant par les bâtiments commerciaux. Ils ont été choisi en 2003 pour la National Design Triennal et travaillent comme conseillers au Los Angeles Forum for Architecture and Urban Design. Ils ont développé dans le domaine de l'art contemporain des idées et projets en coopération avec des artistes. Leurs travaux ont été récompensés internationalement.

El suizo Frank Escher estudió arquitectura en la ETH de Zurich, Ravi Gune Wardena, de Sri Lanka, en Pomona (EEUU) y Florencia. Ambos se unieron en 1995 en una oficina. Su espectro de trabajo alcanza desde la construcción de viviendas, pasando por los edificios comerciales, hasta proyectos públicos en los EEUU y Canadá. En 2003 fueron acogidos en el National Design Triennal y son asesores de Los Angeles Forum for Architecture y de Urban Design. Los arquitectos han desarrollado ideas y proyectos en colaboración con artistas en el ámbito del arte contemporáneo. Sus trabajos han sido premiados a nivel mundial.

Lo svizzero Frank Escher ha studiato architettura al Politecnico (ETH) di Zurigo, Ravi Gune Wardena dallo Sri Lanka a Pomona/USA e Firenze. Nel 1995 i due architetti hanno creato insieme uno studio d'architettura i cui lavori spaziano dai progetti di edilizia residenziale ai complessi commerciali fino ad arrivare alla progettazione dello spazio pubblico realizzata negli Stati Uniti e in Canada. Nel 2003 sono stati registrati nel National Design Triennal; svolgono inoltre attività di consulenza nel Los Angeles Forum for Architecture and Urban Design. Nel panorama artistico contemporaneo hanno sviluppato idee e progetti in stretta collaborazione con artisti. I loro lavori sono stati insigniti di premi e riconoscimenti internazionali.

Fantastic Design Works Inc.

Katsunori Suzuki established the design company Fantastic Design Works in 1986 in Hiroshima and for years the firm has caused a furore with extraordinary designs in the area of gastronomy. Rejecting expressiveness due to its influence by technology, currently, the five employees at Fantastic Design Works are working on the formal reduction of visible tectonics, in order to create a free space for visionary room values. Katsunori Suzuki is a supporter of bio-technics. Instead of today's widely used materials such as concrete and steel, Suzuki would like to use more wood or plant material in construction.

Katsunori Suzuki hat 1986 das Designbüro Fantastic Design Works in Hiroshima gegründet und macht seit Jahren mit außergewöhnlichen Gestaltungen im Bereich der Gastronomie Furore. Den Technik bestimmten Expressionismus ablehnend, arbeitet Fantastic Design Works mit seinen derzeit 5 Mitarbeitern an der formalen Reduktion der sichtbaren Tektonik, um dadurch den Freiraum für visionäre Raumwerte zu eröffnen. Katsunori Suzuki ist ein Befürworter der Biotechnik. Statt der heutzutage genutzten Materialen wie Beton und Stahl würde Suzuki gerne verstärkt mit Holz oder Pflanzenmaterial bauen.

Katsunori Suzuki a fondé en 1986 le bureau de design Fantastic Design Works à Hiroshima et fait fureur depuis des années avec ces aménagements extraordinaires dans le domaine de la restauration. En refusant la technique d'un certain expressionnisme, Fantastic Design Works travaille pour le moment avec ses cinq collaborateurs à la réduction formelle de la tectonique visible, afin d'ouvrir l'espace à des valeurs spatiales visionnaires. Katsunori Suzuki est un partisan de la biotechnique. Au lieu des matériaux utilisés de nos jours comme le béton et l'acier Suzuki aimerait construire beaucoup plus avec du bois ou des matériaux végétaux.

Katsunori Suzuki fundó la oficina de diseño Fantastic Design Works en Hiroshima en 1986 y desde hace años hace furor con excepcionales diseños en el terreno de la gastronomía. Rechazando el expresionismo determinado por la técnica, Fantastic Design Works trabaja, con sus 5 empleados actuales, en la reducción formal de la tectónica visible para abrir, por medio de ello, el espacio libre a los valores del espacio visionarios. Katsunori Suzuki es un precursor de la biotécnica. En lugar de los materiales utilizados actualmente, como el hormigón y el acero, a Suzuki le gustaría construir más con madera o material vegetal.

Katsunori Suzuki ha fondato a Hiroshima lo studio di design Fantastic Design Works nel 1986. Da anni le sue insolite realizzazioni nel settore gastronomico destano grandi entusiasmi. Rifiutando l'espressionismo di ispirazione tecnica, lo studio Fantastic Design Works, che al momento consta di cinque collaboratori, si concentra sulla riduzione formale della funzionalità strutturale per lasciare libero spazio alla sperimentazione dei valori spaziali visionari. Katsunori Suzuki è un sostenitore della biotecnica. Anziché servirsi di materiali attualmente così diffusi quali calcestruzzo e acciaio, Suzuki predilige l'uso del legno e di materiali edilizi di origine vegetale.

gca arquitectes associats

Josep Juanpere Miret studied architecture in Barcelona and Antoni Puig Guasch in Vallés. In 1984, they founded their architectural firm. In the meantime, additional partners, Josep Riu de Martin, Jesús Hernando Fernandez, Arturo de la Maza, Jordi Castañé Portella, Xavier Ballarín Rubio and Lluis Escarmís Costa have joined. They all direct a team of currently more than 50 architects, interior architects and project managers. The firm's main focus is on the renovation and redevelopment of listed buildings, office and commercial buildings, shopping centers and hotel buildings.

Josep Juanpere Miret studierte Architektur in Barcelona, Antoni Puig Guasch in Vallés. 1984 gründeten sie ihr Architekturbüro. Als

Partner sind inzwischen Josep Riu de Martin, Jesús Hernando Fernandez, Arturo de la Maza, Jordi Castañé Portella, Xavier Ballarín Rubio und Lluis Escarmís Costa hinzugekommen. Sie alle stehen einem Team von derzeit über 50 Architekten, Innenarchitekten und Projektmanager vor. Schwerpunkte des Büros sind die Sanierung und Umnutzung von denkmalgeschützten Gebäuden, Büro- und Geschäftsbauten, Einkaufszentren und Hotelbauten.

Josep Juanpere Miret a étudié l'architecture à Barcelone, Antoni Puig Guash à Vallés. Ils ont créé en 1984 leur bureau d'architecture. Entre temps, Josep Riu de Martin, Jesús Hernando Fernandez, Arturo de la Maza, Jordi Castañé Portella, Xavier Ballarín Rubio et Lluis Escarmis Costa les ont rejoints, ils sont tous à la tête d'une équipe qui compte pour le moment plus de 50 architectes, architectes d'intérieur et de directeurs de projets. Le travail du bureau se concentre sur l'assainissement et la transformation de monuments historiques, la construction de bureaux et de magasins, de centres commerciaux et d'hôtels.

Josep Juanpere Miret estudió arquitectura en Barcelona, Antoni Puig Guasch en Vallés. En 1984 fundaron su oficina de arquitectura. Entretanto, se han agregado como socios Josep Riu de Martin, Jesús Hernando Fernández, Arturo de la Maza, Jordi Castañé Portella, Xavier Ballarín Rubio y Lluis Escarmís Costa, estando todos ellos actualmente ante un equipo de más 50 arquitectos, arquitectos de interiores y project managers. Los temas principales de la oficina son los saneamientos y las reutilizaciones de edificios protegidos, las edificaciones comerciales y para oficinas, los centros comerciales y hoteles.

Josep Juanpere Miret ed Antoni Puig Guasch hanno studiato architettura a Barcelona e Vallés rispettivamente. Nel 1984 hanno creato insieme uno studio d'architettura. Ai due fondatori sono andati aggiungendosi diversi soci quali Josep Riu de Martin, Jesús Hernando Fernandez, Arturo de la Maza, Jordi Castañé Portella, Xavier Ballarín Rubio e Lluis Escarmís Costa che sono alla guida di un team che conta attualmente oltre 50 collaboratori fra architetti, architetti d'interni e project manager. Fra le attività di maggiore rilievo dello studio figurano la ristrutturazione e la riqualificazione di edifici posti sotto la tutela dei monumenti storici, complessi di uffi-

ci e complessi commerciali, centri commerciali ed hotel.

gmp – von Gerkan, Marg und Partner

Meinhard von Gerkan, born in Riga in 1935, and Volkwin Marg, born in 1936 in Königsberg, are the founding partners of the architectural firm von Gerkan, Marg und Partner in Hamburg. In the past 35 years, they have planned and built projects in almost all of Germany's major cities and their works decisively influence contemporary architecture. Among their most important buildings are the airports at Berlin-Tegel and Algiers, the exhibition halls in Hanover and Peking or the congress and exhibition center in Nanning, China.

Meinhard von Gerkan, 1935 in Riga geboren, und Volkwin Marg, 1936 in Königsberg geboren, sind Gründer und Partner des Architekturbüros von Gerkan, Marg und Partner in Hamburg. Sie haben in den vergangenen 35 Jahren Projekte in nahezu allen großen Städten Deutschlands geplant und gebaut, und ihre Arbeiten prägen in entscheidendem Maße die zeitgenössische Architektur. Zu den wichtigsten Bauten zählen u. a. die Flughäfen in Berlin-Tegel und Algier, die Messehallen von Hannover und Peking sowie das Kongress- und Ausstellungs-Center in Nanning/China.

Meinhard von Gerkan, né à Riga en 1935, et Volkwin Marg, né à Königsberg en 1936, sont fondateurs et associés du bureau d'architecture von Gerkan, Marg und Partner à Hambourg. Ils ont, lors des 35 dernières années, conçu et réalisé des projets dans presque toutes les grandes villes d'Allemagne et leurs travaux marquent largement l'architecture contemporaine. On compte parmi les constructions les plus importantes entre autre les aéroports de Berlin-Tegel et d'Alger, les halls des expositions de Hanovre et Pékin et le centre des congrès et des expositions de Nanning en Chine.

Meinhard von Gerkan, nacido en 1935 en Riga, y Volkwin Marg, nacido en 1936 en Königsberg, son fundadores y socios de la oficina de arquitectos von Gerkan, Marg und Partner en Hamburgo. En los últimos 35 años han planeado y construido proyectos en casi todas las grandes ciudades de Alemania y sus trabajos marcan la arquitectura contemporánea de manera decisiva. Entre sus edificaciones más importantes cuentan los aeropuertos de Berlin-Tegel y Argelia, los recintos feriales de Hannover y Pekín o el Centro de Congresos y Exposiciones de Nanning (China).

Meinhard von Gerkan, nato a Riga nel 1935, e Volkwin Marg, nato a Königsberg nel 1936, sono fondatori e soci dello studio d'architettura von Gerkan, Marg und Partner con sede ad Amburgo. Negli ultimi 35 anni, von Gerkan e Marg hanno progettato e realizzato opere in quasi tutte le città della Germania, dando impulsi decisivi all'architettura contemporanea. Fra i progetti più importanti sono da annoverare l'aeroporto di Berlin-Tegel ed Algeri, i padiglioni fieristici di Hannover e Pechino o il Centro congressi ed esposizioni di Nanning in Cina.

Grego + Smolenicky Architektur

Jasmin Grego studied art history before she completed her diploma as an architect in 1997 at the ETH (Swiss Technical College) in Zurich. In 1992, she started her own architectural firm with Joseph Smolenicky. Since 2001, she has taught at Basel's College of Higher Education for the Chair of interior architecture, furniture design and scenography and she has been a professor since 2003. Joseph Smolenicky completed his diploma at the ETH in Zurich in 1988, he was research assistant to Prof. Fabio Reinhard and Prof. Hans Kollhoff. He has been a lecturer at the University of Geneva since 1995. The company's main focus is, among other things, in the field of new construction, renovation of existing buildings, urban construction and interiors.

Jasmin Grego hat Kunstgeschichte studiert bevor sie 1997 ihr Diplom als Architektin an der ETH in Zürich machte. Zusammen mit Joseph Smolenicky gründete sie 1992 ihr Architekturbüro. Seit 2001 Lehrtätigkeit an der Fachhochschule Basel am Lehrstuhl für Innenarchitektur, Möbeldesign und Szenografie, seit 2003 als Professorin. Joseph Smolenicky hat 1988 sein Diplom an der ETH Zürich abgelegt, war Assistent bei Prof. Fabio Reinhard und Prof. Hans Kollhoff. Seit 1995 ist er Dozent an der Université de Genève. Der Schwerpunkt des Büros liegt u. a. im Bereich von Neubau, Umbau vorhandener Bauten, des Städtebaus sowie des Interieurs.

Jasmin Grego a d'abord fait des études d'histoire de l'art avant d'étudier et d'obtenir son diplôme d'architecte à l'ETH (Ecole Technique) de Zurich en 1997. Elle s'associe à Joseph Smolencky pour fonder un bureau d'architecture en 1992. Elle enseigne l'architecture d'intérieur, le design de mobilier et la scénographie depuis 2001 à l'Ecole Supérieure de Bâle, depuis 2003 elle y est professeur. Joseph Smolenicky a obtenu son diplôme à l'ETH de Zurich, a été assistant du professeur Fabio Reinhard et du professeur Hans Kollhoff. Depuis 1995, il est maître de conférences à l'Université de Genève. Les points forts du bureau sont les domaines de la construction neuve, de la transformation de bâtiments existants, de l'urbanisme ainsi que de l'architecture intérieure.

Jasmin Grego estudió historia del arte antes de sacar en 1997 su título de arquitecta en la ETH de Zurich. Junto con Joseph Smolenicky fundó en 1992 su oficina de arquitectura. Desde 2001 da clases en la Escuela Técnica Superior de Basilea en la cátedra de arquitectura de interiores, diseño de mobiliario y escenografía, desde 2003 como profesora. Joseph Smolenicky sacó su diploma en la ETH de Zurich en 1988, fue asistente con el profesor Fabio Reinhard y el profesor Hans Kollhoff. Desde 1995 es docente de la Université de Genève. El tema principal de la oficina se halla, entre otros, en el ámbito de la nueva construcción, la reforma de edificios ya existentes, la edificación urbana así como la de los interiores.

Jasmin Grego ha studiato storia dell'arte prima di laurearsi come architetto all'ETH di Zurigo nel 1997. Nel 1992 ha fondato uno studio d'architettura insieme a Joseph Smolenicky. Dal 2001 svolge un'attività didattica presso la Fachhochschule di Basilea nell'Istituto di architettura d'interni, design di mobili e scenografia, dal 2003 in qualità di titolare di cattedra. Joseph Smolenicky ha conseguito la laurea presso l'ETH di Zurigo ed è stato in seguito assistente del prof.

Fabio Reinhard e del prof. Hans Kollhoff. Dal 1995 è docente presso l'Université de Genève. Lo studio è specializzato nella progettazione di edifici nuovi, nella riqualificazione di edifici esistenti, nella progettazione urbanistica nonché nelle realizzazioni d'interior design.

Hideo Horikawa
Architect & Associates

Hideo Horikawa, a well known architect working in Tokyo, is regarded as the father of all Japanese design restaurants. He is the owner of Hideo Horikawa Architect & Associates and he also owns a number of restaurants. His various smaller and larger projects, such as the Coccon Mayu, Davis and Sad Café are, as with many of his colleagues in Japan, influenced by nature and tradition. Hideo Horikawa tries to include this in his projects as a modern form language together with new types of materials.

Hideo Horikawa, ein renommierter, in Tokio tätiger Architekt, gilt als Vater aller japanischen Designlokale. Er ist der Inhaber der Hideo Horikawa Architect & Associates und zugleich Besitzer diverser Restaurants. Seine verschiedenen kleineren und größeren Projekte wie das Coccon Mayu, Davis und Sad Café sind, wie bei vielen seiner Kollegen in Japan, durch die Einflüsse von Natur und Tradition geprägt. Hideo Horikawa versucht, dies in einer modernen Formensprache in Kombination mit neuartigen Materialien in seine Projekte einfließen zu lassen.

Hideo Horikawa, un architecte renommé de Tokyo, est considéré comme le père de tous les bars et restaurants japonais conçus par des designers. Il est propriétaire de Hideo Horikawa Architect & Associates ainsi que de divers restaurants. Ses différents projets, grands et petits, comme le Cocoon Mayu, Davis et Sad Café, sont comme chez beaucoup de ses collègues au Japon, marqués par l'influence de la nature et la tradition. C'est ce que Hideo Horikawa tente, dans une forme de langage moderne en combinaison avec des matériaux nouveaux, de faire passer dans ses projets.

Hideo Horikawa, un arquitecto de prestigio que trabaja en Tokio, está considerado como el padre de todos los locales de diseño japoneses. Es el propietario de Hideo Horikawa Architect & Associates y, al mismo

tiempo, posee diversos restaurantes. Sus diferentes proyectos, mayores y menores, como Coccon Mayu, Davis y Sad Café están marcados, como en el caso de muchos de sus colegas en Japón, por las influencias de la naturaleza y la tradición. Hideo Horikawa intenta hacer afluir esto a sus proyectos en un lenguaje de formas moderno en combinación con materiales modernos.

Hideo Horikawa è un rinomato architetto che opera a Tokio e viene considerato il padre della tipologia di locale design giapponese. È titolare dello studio Hideo Horikawa Architect & Associates e nel contempo proprietario di diversi ristoranti. I suoi svariati lavori quali ad esempio il Coccon Mayu, il Davis e il Sad Café rivelano, come quelli di molti suoi colleghi giapponesi e indipendentemente dalle dimensioni del progetto, un forte legame con la natura e la tradizione. Hideo Horikawa cerca di far confluire questi elementi nei suoi progetti utilizzando un linguaggio espressivo moderno in combinazione con materiali innovativi.

Patrick Jouin

Patrick Jouin studied industrial design in Paris. After graduating, he worked for Thompson Multimedia and Philippe Starck's agency, before he started up his own business in 1998. Like his famous teacher, Jouin has a weakness for clear lines, which are persistently enriched by original details. This works for the Plaza Athénée Restaurant just as much as for a *nutella* spoon and Lille railway station, which he colorfully designed. Patrick Jouin was nominated in Paris in 2003 as the "créateur maison&objet 2003".

Patrick Jouin studierte in Paris Industriedesign. Nach seinem Studium war er für Thompson Multimedia und in der Agentur von Philippe Starck tätig, bevor er sich 1998 selbständig machte. Von seinem berühmten Lehrmeister hat Jouin das Faible für klare Linien mitgebracht, die immer wieder von originellen Details bereichert werden. Das funktioniert beim Restaurant Plaza Athénée ebenso wie bei einem Nutellalöffel bis hin zum Bahnhof von Lille, den er farblich gestaltet hat. Patrick Jouin wurde 2003 in Paris zum „créateur maison&objet 2003" gekürt.

Patrick Jouin a étudié le design industriel à Paris. Après ses études, il a travaillé pour Thompson Multimédia et dans l'agence de

Philippe Starck avant de travailler pour son propre compte. Philipe Jouin a gardé de son célèbre maître un faible pour les lignes claires qui sont toujours enrichies de détails originaux. Cela fonctionne aussi bien pour le restaurant Plaza Athénée que pour une cuillère pour *nutella* que pour la gare de Lille qu'il a conçue tout en couleurs. Patrick Jouin a été élu créateur de l'année au salon « maison&objet 2003 ».

Patrick Jouin estudió diseño industrial en París. Después de su carrera trabajó para Thompson Multimedia y en la agencia de Philippe Starck antes de independizarse en 1998. De su famoso maestro Jouin se trajo la afición por las líneas claras enriquecidas una y otra vez con los detalles originales. Esto funciona para el restaurante Plaza Athénée igual que para una cuchara de *nutella* o la estación de Lille que él configuró en color. Patrick Jouin fue elegido en 2003 en Paris como el "créateur maison&objet 2003".

Patrick Jouin ha studiato a Parigi industrial design. Dopo la laurea ha lavorato per Thompson Multimedia e nell'agenzia di Philippe Starck prima di mettersi in proprio nel 1998. Dal suo celebre maestro, Jouin ha ereditato un debole per le linee pulite arricchite di volta in volta da dettagli originali. Questa è stata la filosofia di fondo nella progettazione tanto del ristorante Plaza Athénée quanto del cucchiaio da *nutella* o della colorata stazione di Lille. Nel 2003 Patrick Jouin ha vinto a Parigi il premio "créateur maison&objet 2003".

Andre Kikoski AIA

Andre Kikoski completed his architectural training in 1995 at Harvard University in Cambridge/USA. Until 2002, he worked for the architectural firms of I. M. Pei, Richard Meier and Costas Kondylis & Partners, before going freelance. His style is a mixture of sobriety and elegance, allied with a sure feeling for colors and materials. Kikoski Architect has been nominated as one of the ten new companies to watch out for by the American Institute of Architects and is described by New York Magazine as belonging to the impressive new guard of ten designers.

Andre Kikoski schloss seine Ausbildung zum Architekten 1995 an der Harvard Universität in Cambridge/USA ab. Bis 2002 war er bei den Architekturbüros I. M. Pei, Richard

Meier und Costas Kondylis & Partners tätig bevor er sich selbständig machte. Sein Stil ist eine Mischung aus Nüchternheit und Eleganz, verbunden mit einem sicheren Gefühl für Farben und Materialien. Kikoski Architect ist als eines der zehn jungen, beachtenswerten Unternehmen vom American Institute of Architects nominiert und vom New York Magazine als zur eindrucksvollen neuen Garde von zehn Designern zählend bezeichnet worden.

Andre Kikoski a achevé sa formation d'architecte à l'Université Harvard à Cambridge/USA. Jusqu'en 2002, il a travaillé dans le bureau d'architecture I. M. Pei, Richard Meier et Costas Kondylis & Partners avant de se mettre à son compte. Son style est un mélange de sobriété et d'élégance associée à un sens affirmé pour les couleurs et les matériaux. Kikoski Architect a été nommé par l'American Institute of Architects comme faisant partie de l'une des dix jeunes entreprises qui retiennent l'attention et le New York Magazine l'a compté parmi les dix designers de la remarquable nouvelle garde.

Andre Kikoski concluyó su formación como arquitecto en 1995 en la Harvard University de Cambridge (EEUU). Hasta 2002 trabajó en las oficinas de arquitectura I. M. Pei, Richard Meier y Costas Kondylis & Partners antes de hacerse independiente. Su estilo es una mezcla de sobriedad y elegancia ligado a un sentido seguro por los colores y los materiales. Kikorski Architect ha sido nominado por el American Institute of Architects como una de las diez empresas jóvenes más notables y denominada por el New York Magazine como perteneciente a la nueva elite impresionante de diez diseñadores.

Andre Kikoski ha concluso i suoi studi di architettura presso la Harvard University di Cambridge/USA nel 1995. In seguito ha iniziato a lavorare presso gli studi di architettura I. M. Pei, Richard Meier e Costas Kondylis & Partners finché ha deciso di mettersi in proprio. Il suo stile si contraddistingue per la combinazione di sobrietà ed eleganza unite ad un istinto sicuro che lo guida nella scelta di colori e materiali. Lo studio Kikorski Architect è stato nominato dall'American Institute of Architects fra le dieci giovani aziende degne di nota. Kikoski stesso è stato designato dal New York Magazine come uno dei dieci designer di maggior spicco della nuova guardia.

Yasuhiro Koichi
Design Studio SPIN

Yasuhiro Koichi is the creative head, chief shareholder and managing director of Design Studio SPIN, one of Tokyo's most important design and architectural firms. The design studio is the creator of unique restaurant and interior architecture, especially in Asia. Bars and restaurants in the Inter-Continental MidPlaza Jakarta, at Sentosa Resort and in the Sukhothai Hotel Bangkok count among the numerous projects completed by Studio SPIN.

Yasuhiro Koichi ist der kreative Kopf, Hauptgesellschafter und Geschäftsführer bei Design Studio SPIN, einem der bedeutendsten Design- und Architekturbüros in Tokio. Das Designstudio ist der Schöpfer einer einmaligen Restaurant- und Innenarchitektur speziell auf dem asiatischen Kontinent. Zu den zahlreichen von Studio SPIN realisierten Projekten gehören Bars und Restaurants im InterContinental MidPlaza Jakarta, im Sentosa Resort und im Sukhothai Hotel Bangkok.

Yasuhiro Koichi est la tête créatrice, le principal actionnaire et le directeur du Design Studio SPIN, un des bureaux de design et d'architecture les plus importants de Tokyo. Le studio de design crée une architecture de restaurant et d'intérieur unique spécialement sur le continent asiatique. Parmi les nombreux projets réalisés par le Studio SPIN, on trouve des bars et restaurants à l'InterContinental MidPlaza à Jakarta, au Sentosa Resort et Sukhothai Hotel à Bangkok.

Yasuhiro Koichi es el cerebro creador, el socio principal y gerente de Design Studio SPIN, una de las oficinas de diseño y arquitectura más importantes de Tokio. El estudio de diseño es el creador de una arquitectura de restaurantes e interiores excepcional especialmente en el continente asiático. Entre los numerosos proyectos realizados por Studio SPIN se cuentan bares y restaurantes en el InterContinental MidPlaza de Yakarta, el Sentosa Resort y el Sukhothai Hotel de Bangkok.

Yasuhiro Koichi è la mente creativa nonché il socio maggioritario e l'amministratore dello studio Design Studio SPIN, uno dei più importanti studi di design e di architettura di Tokio. Lo studio ha lanciato uno stile di architettura gastronomica e d'interni creata appositamente per il continente asiatico. Fra i numerosi progetti realizzati da Studio SPIN figurano bar e ristoranti dell'InterContinental MidPlaza Jakarta, nel Sentosa Resort nonché nel Sukhothai Hotel Bangkok.

Koning Eizenberg Architecture

Koning Eizenberg Architecture was founded in 1981 by Julie Eizenberg and Hank Koning and is mainly active in the vicinity of Santa Monica. The main areas of work are private and public buildings as well as hotel and shop designs. Inspirations such as Frank O. Gehry and Charles Moore influence their imaginative, landscape references and humanist architectures. In 1989, the studio was nominated as one of 30 leading architectural practices worldwide, in 1987, it was awarded the "Progressive Architecture First Award", in 1994 the "National AIA Honor Award" and in 2004 honored as the "Residential Architect Firm of the Year".

Koning Eizenberg Architecture wurde 1981 von Julie Eizenberg und Hank Koning gegründet und wirkt hauptsächlich im Umkreis von Santa Monica. Private und öffentliche Bauten sowie Hotel- und Shopdesigns zählen zu den Haupttätigkeitsgebieten. Vorbilder wie Frank O. Gehry und Charles Moore prägen ihre fantasievollen, landschaftsbezogenen und menschenorientierten Architekturen. Das Büro wurde 1989 zu den 30 weltweit führenden Architekturbüros gewählt, 1987 mit dem „Progressive Architecture First Award", 1994 mit dem „National AIA Honor Award" ausgezeichnet und 2004 als „Residential Architect Firm of the Year" gewürdigt.

Koning Eizenberg Architecture a été crée en 1981 par Julie Eizenberg et Hank Koning et travaille principalement dans la région de Santa Monica. Leurs activités principales concernent des bâtiments privés ou publics comme le design d'hôtel ou de boutiques. Leurs architectures pleines de fantaisie, humaines et tenant compte du paysage sont imprégnées de l'esprit de modèles comme Frank O. Gehry et Charles Moore. Le bureau a été choisi en 1989 comme faisant partie des 30 bureaux d'architecture les plus importants du monde. Il a été récompensé en 1987 par le prix du « Progressive Architecture First Award », en 1994 par « National AIA Honor Award » et en 2004 a été consacré en 2004 comme « Residential Architect Firm of the Year ».

Koning Eizenberg Architecture fue fundada en 1981 por Julie Eizenberg y Hank Koning y actúa principalmente en los alrededores de Santa Mónica. Entre los campos principales de actividad se cuentan las edificaciones privadas y públicas así como los diseños de hoteles y tiendas. Modelos como Frank O. Gehry y Charles Moore caracterizan sus arquitecturas llenas de fantasía, referidas al paisaje y orientadas al ser humano. En 1989 la oficina fue elegida entre las 30 oficinas de arquitectura más importantes mundialmente, en 1987 fue distinguida con el "Progressive Architecture First Award", en 1994 con el "National AIA Honor Award" y en 2004 reconocida como "Residential Architect Firm of the Year".

Julie Eizenberg e Hank Koning sono i fondatori dello studio Koning Eizenberg Architecture, creato nel 1981, che opera soprattutto nella regione di Santa Monica. L'edilizia pubblica e privata nonché l'hotel design e lo shop design sono solo alcune delle aree di maggior rilievo in cui lo studio è andato specializzandosi. Modelli quali Frank O. Gehry e Charles Moore influenzano le creative progettazioni architettoniche firmate Koning Eizenberg che rivelano un forte legame con il territorio ed una spiccata sensibilità per le esigenze dell'uomo. Nel 1989 lo studio è stato designato fra i 30 studi di architettura più quotati a livello internazionale. È seguito il conferimento di ulteriori riconoscimenti quali il "Progressive Architecture First Award" (1987), il "National AIA Honor Award" (1994) nonché il "Residential Architect Firm of the Year" (2004).

Atelier Kunc

The Kunc Atelier was founded in 1989 by Michal Kunc and consists of a group of close partners from the areas of architecture, interiors and design. Since its establishment, the atelier looks after clients from culture, industry and technology and offers services in the area of interior architecture for offices and restaurants, for conferences, staging different themes, exhibitions and trade fair appearances for international companies such as Henkel, Nissan and VW.

Das Atelier Kunc wurde 1989 von Michal Kunc gegründet und besteht aus einer Gruppe von festen Partnern aus den Bereichen Architektur, Interieur und Design. Seit seiner Gründung betreut das Atelier Kunden aus Kultur, Industrie und Technologie und bietet Leistungen im Bereich von Innenarchitektur für Büros und Gastronomie, von Veranstaltungen, Themeninszenierungen, Ausstellungen und Messeauftritten für internationale Unternehmen wie Henkel, Nissan und VW.

L'Atelier Kunc a été créé en 1989 par Michal Kunc et est composé aujourd'hui d'un groupe de partenaires stables venant des domaines de l'architecture, de l'architecture d'intérieur et du design. Depuis sa création l'Atelier a des clients dans les secteurs de la culture, l'industrie et la technologie. Il exerce ses compétences dans le domaine de l'architecture d'intérieur pour des bureaux et restaurants, de l'organisation de manifestations, de la mise en scène de thèmes, des expositions et des représentations sur les grandes foires d'entreprises internationales comme Henkel, Nissan et VW.

El taller Kunc fue fundado en 1989 por Michal Kunc y consta de un grupo de socios fijos provenientes de los terrenos de la arquitectura, el interior y el diseño. Desde su fundación el taller asesora a clientes de la cultura, industria y tecnología y ofrece prestaciones en el ámbito de la arquitectura de interiores para oficinas y gastronomía; en el ámbito de los actos, las escenificaciones temáticas, exposiciones y presentaciones en ferias para empresas internacionales como Henkel, Nissan y Volkswagen.

Fondato da Michal Kunc nel 1989, l'Atelier Kunc è composto da un gruppo di collaboratori fissi esperti nei settori architettura, interior design e design. Fin dalla sua creazione, l'Atelier è andato specializzandosi nella realizzazione di progetti commissionati da clienti del comparto culturale, industriale e tecnologico. Le soluzioni offerte spaziano dalle proposte d'interior design per uffici e la gastronomia all'event design, alle scenografie a tema, agli allestimenti espositivi e fieristici per gruppi internazionali quali per esempio Henkel, Nissan und VW.

Lazzarini Pickering Architetti / Tanner Architects

Claudio Lazzarini, born in 1953 in Rome, studied architecture at Rome's La Sapienza University. Carl Pickering, born in 1960 in Sydney, arrived in Italy in 1980 and studied in Venice. Both architects have been working together since 1983. Their areas of work are new buildings, renovations and restorations as well as art consultancy. Tanner Architects in Sydney represent the disciplines of architecture and design. They were awarded over 30 prizes and distinctions for their work, among others, by UNESCO and the National Trust for exemplary renovations, by the Institute of Architects for the renovation of Sydney's city hall.

Claudio Lazzarini, 1953 in Rom geboren, studierte Architektur an der Universität La Sapienza in Rom. Carl Pickering, 1960 in Sydney geboren, kam 1980 nach Italien und studierte in Venedig. Seit 1983 arbeiten beide Architekten zusammen; ihre Tätigkeitsbereiche sind Neubauten, Sanierungen und Restaurierungen sowie künstlerische Beratung. Tanner Architects aus Sydney stehen für die Disziplinen Architektur und Design. Für ihre Arbeit erhielten sie über 30 Preise und Auszeichnungen, u. a. von der UNESCO und dem National Trust für vorbildliche Renovierungen, vom Institute of Architects für die Renovierung der Stadthalle von Sydney.

Claudio Lazzarini, né à Rome en 1953, a étudié l'architecture à l'Université de La Sapienza à Rome. Carl Pickering, né à Sydney en 1960, est arrivé en Italie en 1980 et a étudié à Venise. Les deux architectes travaillent ensemble depuis 1983 ; leurs domaines sont les nouvelles constructions, l'assainissement et la restauration ainsi que le conseil artistique. Le bureau Tanner Architects de Sydney représente les disciplines architecture et design. Ils ont reçu pour leur travail plus de trente prix et distinctions, entre autre de l'UNESCO et du National Trust pour leurs travaux exemplaires de rénovation, de l'Institute of Architects pour la rénovation de la halle municipale de Sydney.

Claudio Lazzarini, nacido en Roma en 1953, estudió arquitectura en la Universidad La Sapienza en Roma. Carl Pickering, nacido en Sydney en 1960, llegó a Italia en 1980 y estudió en Venecia. Ambos arquitectos trabajan juntos desde 1983; sus campos de actividad son los edificios nuevos, las reha-

bilitaciones y restauraciones así como la asesoría artística. Los Tanner Architects de Sydney son un sinónimo de las disciplinas de la arquitectura y del diseño. Por su trabajo han recibido más de 30 premios y distinciones, entre otros de la UNESCO y del National Trust por sus reformas ejemplares, del Institute of Architects por la reforma del auditorio municipal de Sydney.

Claudio Lazzarini è nato a Roma nel 1953 dove ha studiato architettura all'Università La Sapienza. Carl Pickering, nato a Sydney nel 1960, si è trasferito in Italia nel 1980 e ha studiato a Venezia. Dal 1983 i due architetti lavorano assieme, occupandosi soprattutto di progetti architettonici, restauri, ristrutturazioni nonché consulenza artistica. I nomi dei titolari dello studio Tanner Architects di Sydney sono sinonimi delle discipline architettura e design. Per i progetti realizzati lo studio è già stato insignito di oltre 30 premi e riconoscimenti, fra i quali quelli dell'UNESCO e del National Trust per opere di restauro esemplare e dell'Institute of Architects per la ristrutturazione del palazzo per manifestazioni culturali di Sydney.

Lewis. Tsurumaki. Lewis LTL architects

The cooperation of the brothers Paul and David J. Lewis with Marc Tsurumaki began in 1993. This resulted in the emergence in 2003 of Lewis.Tsurumaki. Lewis LTL architects as an architectural and research company, whose goal is to achieve as many different projects as possible. The firm's work ranges from large building projects, standard-setting prototypes to theoretical projects and museum installations to exhibition design. Marc Tsurumaki teaches architecture at Columbia University. David J. Lewis is the Director of the Master Arch Program at the Parsons School of Design in New York.

1993 begann die Zusammenarbeit der Brüder Paul und David J. Lewis mit Marc Tsurumaki. Daraus ging 2003 Lewis.Tsurumaki. Lewis LTL architects als Architektur- und Forschungsgesellschaft hervor, die sich zum Ziel gesetzt hat, möglichst viele unterschiedliche

Projekte zu realisieren. Die Arbeiten des Büros reichen von großen Gebäudeprojekten und maßstäblichen Prototypen über theoretische Projekte und Museumsinstallationen bis hin zu Ausstellungsdesign. Marc Tsurumaki lehrt Architektur an der Columbia University. David J. Lewis ist der Direktor des Master Arch Program an der Parsons School of Design in New York.

C'est en 1993 qu'a commencé la coopération des frères Paul et David J. Lewis avec Marc Tsurumaki. De là est né la société d'architecture et de recherche Lewis. Tsurumaki.Lewis LTL architects, qui s'est donné pour but de réaliser autant de projets différents que possible. Les travaux du bureau d'architecture vont de la réalisation de grands projets de bâtiments et de prototypes grandeur nature à la conception d'expositions en passant par des projets théoriques et des installations de musées. Marc Tsurumaki enseigne l'architecture à l'Université de Kolumbia. Davis J. Lewis est directeur du programme Master Arch à l'Ecole de Design Parson à New York.

En 1993 comenzó la colaboración de los hermanos Paul y David J. Lewis con Marc Tsurumaki. De ello resultó en 2003 Lewis. Tsurumaki.Lewis LTL architects como una sociedad de arquitectura e investigación que se ha impuesto como meta realizar tantos proyectos distintos como sea posible. Los trabajos de la oficina van de los grandes proyectos de edificios y los prototipos a escala pasando por los proyectos teóricos y las instalaciones de museos hasta el diseño de exposiciones. Marc Tsurumaki da clases de arquitectura en la Columbia University. David J. Lewis es director del Master Arch Program en la Parsons School of Design de Nueva York.

La collaborazione fra i fratelli Paul e David J. Lewis e Marc Tsurumaki è iniziata nel 1993. Nel 2003 essa ha dato origine allo studio di progettazione e ricerca architettonica Lewis. Tsurumaki. Lewis LTL architects, che persegue l'obiettivo di differenziare quanto possibile i progetti curati. I lavori già realizzati da questo studio spaziano dai progetti architettonici e dai prototipi in scala ai progetti teorici e agli allestimenti museali fino ad arrivare all'exhibition design. Marc Tsurumaki insegna architettura alla Columbia University. David J. Lewis è direttore del Master Arch Program alla Parsons School of Design di New York.

Lohan Caprile Goettsch Architects

Lohan Associates was the result of the partnership, which was formed in 1962 between Mies van der Rohe and Dirk Lohan. In 1973, Joseph Caprile finished his architectural studies at the University of Illinois. In 1981, he joined Lohan Associates, where he has been a partner since 1990. In 1967, James Goettsch graduated in architecture at Iowa State University. In 1992, he joined Lohan Associates and works there as design chief. In 2002, the office was renamed as Lohan Caprile Goettsch Architects and today it employs 45 architects, interior architects and graphic designers.

Lohan Associates ging aus der 1962 geschlossenen Partnerschaft zwischen Mies van der Rohe und Dirk Lohan hervor. Joseph Caprile beendete 1973 sein Architekturstudium an der University of Illinois. 1981 begann er bei Lohan Associates, seit 1990 ist er dort Partner. James Goettsch schloss 1967 sein Architekturstudium an der Iowa State University ab. 1992 trat er bei Lohan Associates ein und ist dort als Designvorstand tätig. 2002 wurde das Büro in Lohan Caprile Goettsch Architects umbenannt und beschäftigt heute 45 Architekten, Innenarchitekten und Grafikdesigner.

Lohan Associates est né en 1962 de la coopération entre Mies van der Rohe et Dirk Lohan. Joseph Caprile a terminé en 1973 ses études d'architecture à l'Université de l'Illinois. Il a commencé à travailler chez Lohan Associates en 1981, depuis 1990 il est devenu un des partenaires de l'entreprise. James Goettsch a terminé en 1967 ses études d'architecture à l'Université de l'état d'Iowa. Il entre chez Lohan Associates en 1992 où il est responsable du design dans le comité de direction. En 2002 le bureau a pris le nom de Lohan Caprile Goettsch Architects et emploie aujourd'hui 45 architectes, architectes d'intérieur et graphistes.

Lohan Associates resultó de la cooperación convenida en 1962 entre Mies van der Rohe y Dirk Lohan. Joseph Caprile terminó en 1973 su carrera de arquitectura en la University of Illinois. En 1981 comenzó en Lohan Associates, desde 1990 es socio allí. James Goettsch acabó en 1967 su carrera de arquitectura en la Iowa State University. En 1992 entró en Lohan Associates y trabaja allí en la directiva de diseño. En 2002 la oficina cambió su nombre en Lohan Caprile

Goettsch Architects y actualmente emplea a 45 arquitectos, arquitectos de interiores y diseñadores gráficos.

Lo studio Lohan Associates è nato dal sodalizio iniziato nel 1962 fra Mies van der Rohe e Dirk Lohan. Joseph Caprile ha completato i suoi studi di architettura presso la University of Illinois nel 1973. Nel 1981 ha iniziato la sua attività presso lo studio Lohan Associates, di cui è diventato socio nel 1990. James Goettsch ha conseguito la laurea in architettura presso la Iowa State University nel 1967. Nel 1992 è entrato nello studio Lohan Associates presso il quale svolge la funzione di capo design. Nel 2002 lo studio ha cambiato nome trasformandosi in Lohan Caprile Goettsch Architects. Attualmente vi lavorano 45 collaboratori fra architetti, architetti d'interni e graphic designer.

Lynch / Eisinger / Design (L/E/D)

Christian Lynch and Simon Eisinger met during their architectural studies at Columbia University in New York. Lynch finished his studies in 1990 at the University of California and after that he worked, among others, for Stanley Saitowitz and Franklin D. Israel Design Associates. Eisinger completed his studies in 1990 at the Massachusetts Institute of Technology with a distinction for his excellent performances. Afterwards, he worked for Behnisch & Partner, I. M. Pei Cobb Freed and Gabellini. Lynch and Eisinger have worked together since 1997. In 1999, they founded Lynch / Eisinger / Design (L/E/D) in New York.

Christian Lynch und Simon Eisinger lernten sich während ihres Architekturstudiums an der Columbia University in New York kennen. Lynch beendete sein Studium 1990 an der University of California und war danach u. a. bei Stanley Saitowitz und Franklin D. Israel Design Associates tätig. Eisinger schloss sein Studium 1990 am Massachusetts Institute of Technology mit einer Auszeichnung für seine herausragenden Leistungen ab. Danach war er bei Behnisch & Partner, I. M. Pei Cobb Freed und Gabellini tätig. Seit 1997 arbeiteten Lynch und Eisinger zusammen. 1999 gründeten sie in New York Lynch / Eisinger / Design (L/E/D).

Christian Lynch et Simon Eisinger se sont connus pendant leurs études à l'Université de Columbia de New York. Lynch a terminé ses études en 1990 à l'Université de Californie et a travaillé ensuite entre autre chez Stanley Saitowitz et Franklin D. Israel Design Associates. Eisinger a terminé ses études en 1990 à l'Institut de technologie du Massachusetts et a été récompensé pour ses remarquables travaux. Il a travaillé ensuite chez Behnisch & Partner, I. M. Pei Cobb Freed et Gabellini. Lynch et Eisinger travaillent ensemble depuis 1997. Ils ont fondé en 1999 à New York Lynch / Eisinger / Design (L/E/D).

Christian Lynch y Simon Eisinger se conocieron durante su carrera de arquitectura en la Columbia University en Nueva York. Lynch terminó su carrera en 1990 en la University of California y después trabajó, entre otros, para Stanley Saitowitz y Franklin D. Israel Design Associates. Eisinger terminó su carrera en 1990 en el Institute of Technology de Massachusetts con una distinción por sus excepcionales rendimientos. Después de ello trabajó para Behnisch & Partner, I. M. Pei Cobb Freed y Gabellini. A partir de 1997 Lynch y Eisinger trabajaron juntos. En 1999 fundaron Lynch / Eisinger / Design (L/E/D) en Nueva York.

Christian Lynch e Simon Eisinger si sono conosciuti durante gli studi di architettura compiuti presso la Columbia University a New York. Lynch ha completato il suo corso di studi presso la University of California e ha lavorato in seguito presso lo studio Stanley Saitowitz und Franklin D. Israel Design Associates. Eisinger ha completato i suoi studi presso il Massachusetts Institute of Technology ottenendo un riconoscimento per meriti eccezionali. In seguito ha iniziato la sua attività lavorativa presso lo studio Behnisch & Partner, I. M. Pei Cobb Freed e Gabellini. La collaborazione di Lynch e Eisinger è iniziata nel 1997 ed ha portato, nel 1999, alla fondazione dello studio Lynch / Eisinger / Design (L/E/D) a New York.

Dodd Mitchell Design Associates

Dodd Mitchell is an interior architect and founder of Dodd Mitchell Design Associates. He directs architects and designers, who previously worked for Gehry Partners, Ian Schrager, Hirsch Bedner, Richard Meier and other leading companies. Dodd Mitchell has a number of illustrious projects to show in the areas of interior design and architecture, among them, the restaurants Dolce Enoteca, Katana, Boa, Zen Grill and Linq restaurant in Los Angeles, the Crescent Hotel in Beverly Hills, the Huntley Hotel in Santa Monica and the Hollywood Roosevelt Hotel, as well as the Chrysler Lounge at the Sundance Film Festival.

Dodd Mitchell ist Innenarchitekt und Begründer der Dodd Mitchel Design Associates. Unter seiner Führung arbeiten Architekten und Designer, die zuvor bei Gehry Partners, Ian Schrager, Hirsch Bedner, Richard Meier und anderen namhaften Unternehmen tätig waren. Im Bereich Interieur Design und Architektur hat Dodd Mitchel eine Reihe illustrer Projekte vorzuweisen, darunter die Restaurants Dolce Enoteca, Katana, Boa, Zen Grill und Linq in Los Angeles, die Hotelprojekte Crescent Hotel in Beverly Hills, das Huntley Hotel in Santa Monica und das Hollywood Roosevelt Hotel sowie die Chrysler Lounge beim Sundance Film Festival.

Dodd Mitchell est architecte d'intérieur et fondateur de Dodd Mitchell Design Associates. Sous sa direction travaillent des architectes et designers qui ont travaillé auparavant chez Gehry Partners, Ian Schrager, Hirsch Bedner, Richard Meier et dans d'autres entreprises renommées. Dans le domaine du design d'intérieur et de l'architecture Dodd Mitchell a montré ses capacités dans bon nombre de projets illustres, parmi lesquels les restaurants Dolce Enoteca, Katana, Boa, Zen Grill, et Linq à Los Angeles, le projet d'hôtel Crescent Hotel à Beverly Hills, le Huntley Hotel à Santa Monica et le Hollywood Roosevelt Hotel ainsi que la Lounge Chrysler au Festival du film Sundance.

Dodd Mitchell es arquitecto de interiores y cofundador de Dodd Mitchel Design Associates. Bajo su dirección trabajan arquitectos y diseñadores que anteriormente trabajaron para Gehry Partners, Ian Schrager, Hirsch Bedner, Richard Meier y otros prestigiosos empresarios. Dodd Mitchell puede hacer gala de una serie de proyectos ilustres en el ámbito del diseño de interiores y la arquitectura, entre ellos, los restaurantes Dolce Enoteca, Katana, Boa, Zen Grill y Linq en Los Ángeles, los proyectos de hoteles Crescent Hotel en Beverly Hills, el Huntley Hotel en Santa Mónica y el Hollywood Roosevelt Hotel así como el Chrysler Lounge en el Sundance Film Festival.

Dodd Mitchell è architetto d'interni e fondatore dello studio Dodd Mitchel Design Associates. Sotto la sua guida operano architetti e designer che hanno già lavorato presso gli studi Gehry Partners, Ian Schrager, Hirsch Bedner, Richard Meier ed altre aziende rinomate. Nel campo dell'interior design e dell'architettura Dodd Mitchel vanta una serie di progetti illustri fra cui vanno annoverati i ristoranti Dolce Enoteca, Katana, Boa, Zen Grill e Linq a Los Angeles, la progettazione d'hotel quali il Crescent Hotel a Beverly Hills, l'Huntley Hotel a Santa Monica e l'Hollywood Roosevelt Hotel nonché la realizzazione del Chrysler Lounge in occasione del Sundance Film Festival.

Ontwerpwerk
multidisciplinary design

Guus Boudestein and Ed Annik are two of the directors for Ontwerpwerk multidisciplinary design. The firm employs about 30 employees, who form teams for various specialisms such as graphic design, interior architecture, industrial design and new media design. The interior architects are responsible for consulting and design on themes related to interiors, exhibitions and furniture design, such as for the Royal Theater in Amsterdam or the Guthschmidt Jewelry Gallery. The design team works for companies such as Driade, Authentics and Droog.

Guus Boudestein und Ed Annik sind zwei der Direktoren von Ontwerpwerk multidisciplinary design. Das Büro beschäftigt rund 30 Mitarbeiter, die Teams für verschiedene Arbeitsschwerpunkte wie Grafikdesign, Innenarchitektur, Industriedesign und New Media Design bilden. Die Innenarchitekten sind zuständig für die Beratung und Gestaltung bei Themen rund um den Innenraum, Ausstellungen und das Möbel-Design, wie z. B. in Amsterdam für das Royal Theater oder die Guthschmidt Schmuckgalerie, das Design-Team arbeitet für Firmen wie Driade, Authentics und Droog.

Guus Boudestein et Ed Annik sont deux des directeurs du Ontwepwerk multidisciplinary design. Le bureau emploie environ 30 collaborateurs qui forment des équipes qui travaillent particulièrement dans les domaines du design graphique, de l'architecture d'intérieur, du design industriel et du New Media Design. Les architectes d'intérieur sont responsables du conseil et de la conception en ce qui concerne les thèmes touchant à l'espace intérieur, les expositions et le design de meubles, comme par exemple à Amsterdam pour le Royal Theater ou la galerie de bijoux Guthschmidt, l'équipe du département design travaille pour des firmes comme Driade, Authentics et Droog.

Guus Boudestein y Ed Annik son dos de los directores de Ontwerpwerk multidisciplinary design. La oficina emplea a alrededor de 30 empleados que forman equipos para diferentes temas principales de trabajo como el diseño gráfico, la arquitectura de interiores, el diseño industrial y el diseño new media. Los arquitectos de interiores son responsables de la asesoría y la creación en temas sobre interiores, exposiciones y diseño de muebles, como por ejemplo en Amsterdam para el Royal Theater o la galería de joyas Guthschmidt, el equipo de diseño trabaja para empresas como Driade, Authentics y Droog.

Guus Boudestein e Ed Annik sono due dei direttori dello studio Ontwerpwerk multidisciplinary design. Nello studio lavorano circa 30 collaboratori suddivisi in team di lavoro specializzati rispettivamente in graphic design, architettura d'interni, industrial design e new media design. Gli architetti d'interni svolgono attività di consulenza e progettazione curandosi di tutti gli aspetti correlati all'interior design, all'exhibition design e al design di mobili, come ad esempio nei progetti realizzati ad Amsterdam per il Royal Theater o la galleria di gioielli Guthschmidt; il team di design lavora inoltre per ditte quali Driade, Authentics e Droog.

Oda Pälmke

Oda Pälmke was born in Flensburg in 1965. After studying architecture at the art school (HdK) in Berlin, she gained experience as a project leader for the Kollhoff and Timmermann studio, before starting her own company in 1994. From 2002, she worked partly on a partnership project with Tobias Engelschall and is a founding member of the group SHRINKtoFIT. She was a scientific associate of the Bauhaus University in Weimar, guest professor at Virginia Tech University, as well as CUJAE University, Havanna and at the EPFL, Lausanne. She is currently working as a guest professor for design at the Academy of Visual Arts (HfbK), Hamburg.

Oda Pälmke wurde 1965 in Flensburg geboren. Nach ihrem Architekturstudium an der HdK Berlin hat sie als Projektleiterin im Büro Kollhoff und Timmermann Erfahrung gesammelt, bevor sie 1994 ihr eigenes Büro eröffnete. Seit 2002 arbeitet sie teilweise in Projektpartnerschaft mit Tobias Engelschall und ist Gründungsmitglied der Gruppe SHRINKtoFIT. Sie war wissenschaftliche Mitarbeiterin an der Bauhaus-Universität Weimar, Gastprofessorin an der Virginia Tech University, an der Universität CUJAE, Havanna und an der EPFL, Lausanne. Derzeit ist sie Gastprofessorin für Entwurf an der HfbK Hamburg.

Oda Pälmke est née à Flensburg en 1965. Après ses études d'architecture à l'Ecole d'Art (HdK) de Berlin, elle acquiert de l'expérience en tant que directrice de projets dans le bureau Kollhoff et Timmermann, avant d'ouvrir en 1994 son propre bureau. Depuis 2002, elle travaille en partie en collaboration sur des projets avec Tobias Engelschall et est membre de la fondation du groupe SHRINKtoFIT. Elle a été collaboratrice scientifique à l'Université du Bauhaus de Weimar, professeur invitée à la Virginia Tech University, à l'Université CUJAE de La Havane, et à la EPFL de Lausanne. Elle est maintenant professeur invitée à l'Ecole d'Art de Hambourg (HfbK).

Oda Pälmke nació en 1965 en Flensburg. Tras su carrera de arquitectura en la Universidad de Artes de Berlín (HdK) reunió experiencia como directora de proyectos en la oficina Kollhoff y Timmermann antes de abrir su propia oficina en 1994. Desde 2002 trabaja en parte en cooperación de proyectos con Tobias Engelschall y es miembro fundador del grupo SHRINKtoFIT. Fue colaboradora científica en la Universidad Bauhaus de Weimar, profesora invitada en la Virginia Tech University, en la Universidad CUJAE de La Habana y en la EPFL de Lausana. Actualmente es profesora invitada de diseño en la Universidad de Artes Plásticas de Hamburgo (HfbK).

Oda Pälmke è nata a Flensburg nel 1965. Dopo aver completato gli studi di architettura presso la Università delle Arti (HdK) di Berlino, ha fatto esperienza lavorando dapprima come responsabile di progetti presso lo studio Kollhoff e Timmermann fino a quando, nel 1994, ha fondato il suo studio d'architettura. Dal 2002 ha realizzato dei progetti insieme a Tobias Engelschall ed è membro fondatore del gruppo SHRINKto-FIT. È stata collaboratrice scientifica presso la Bauhaus-Universität di Weimar, professore ospite alla Virginia Tech University nonché presso l'istituto CUJAE dell'Havana e EPFL di Losanna. Attualmente è professore ospite di progettazione presso Università delle Arti Figurative (HdK) ad Amburgo.

de Picciotto und Wittorf Architekten

The native New Yorker, Charles de Picciotto, graduated in architecture from Hanover University and the School of Visual Arts in New York. From 1991 to 1997 he worked for von Gerkan, Marg und Partner in Hamburg, in 1997 he established the Picciotto Architecture Atelier. Charles de Picciotto is the Chairman of the Federal Association of German Architects in Hamburg. In 2001, he formed a partnership with Wittorf Architects. Lars Wittorf was born in Neumünster, studied architecture in Hamburg and from 1996 until the merger, he ran his own firm under his name.

Der in New York geborene Charles de Picciotto absolvierte sein Architekturstudium an der Universität Hannover und der School of Visual Arts in New York. Von 1991 bis 1997 arbeitet er bei von Gerkan, Marg und Partner in Hamburg, 1997 gründete er das Architektur-Atelier de Picciotto. Charles de Picciotto ist Vorstand des Bundesverbands Deutscher Architekten, Hamburg. 2001 schloss er sich mit Wittorf Architekten zu einem gemeinsamen Büro zusammen. Lars Wittorf ist in Neumünster geboren, studierte Architektur in Hamburg und hatte seit 1996 bis zum Zusammenschluss ein gleichnamiges Büro.

Charles de Picciotto, qui est né à New York, a fait ses études d'architecture à l'Université de Hambourg et à la School of Visual Arts de New York. Il a travaillé de 1991 à 1997 chez von Gerkan, Marg und Partner à Hambourg et a fondé l'atelier d'architecture de Picciotto Hambourg en 1997. Charles de Picciotto est membre du comité directeur de la Fédération des architectes allemands de Hambourg. En 2001 il s'associe à Wittorf Architekten pour créer un bureau. Lars Wittorf est

né à Neumünster, il a étudié l'architecture à Hambourg et avait, jusqu'à ce qu'il s'associe à Charles de Picciotto, depuis 1996 un bureau portant son propre nom.

Charles de Picciotto, nacido en Nueva York, estudió su carrera de arquitectura en la Universidad de Hannover y en la School of Visual Arts en Nueva York. De 1991 a 1997 trabajó para von Gerkan, Marg und Partner en Hamburgo, en 1997 fundó el taller de arquitectura de Picciotto. Charles de Picciotto está en la directiva de la Asociación Federal de Arquitectos Alemanes de Hamburgo. En 2001 se unió con Wittorf Architekten en una oficina conjunta. Lars Wittorf nació en Neumünster, estudió arquitectura en Hamburgo y, desde 1996 hasta la fusión, tuvo la oficina del mismo nombre.

Nato a New York, Charles de Picciotto ha studiato architettura all'università di Hannover e alla School of Visual Arts di New York. Dopo aver lavorato presso lo studio von Gerkan, Marg und Partner ad Amburgo dal 1991 al 1997, si è messo in proprio nel 1997 dando vita all'Architektur Atelier de Picciotto. Charles de Picciotto è presidente della federazione degli architetti tedeschi Bundesverbands Deutscher Architekten Hamburg. Nel 2001 al preesistente studio Wittorf Architekten subentra lo studio fondato da de Picciotto e Wittorf. Lars Wittorf, nato a Neumünster, ha studiato architettura ad Amburgo e fino alla creazione di uno studio con de Picciotto nel 1996 era già titolare di un omonimo studio di architettura.

Project Orange

Project Orange is an architectural and design firm founded in 1997 in London by James Soane and Christopher Ash. The company emerged from a loosely formed group of young architects in 1992. Both studied architecture at Cambridge. Ash then worked for different well-known firms such as Conran & Partners or Paul Hyett, whilst Soane first taught for nine years at Kingston University before he also joined Conran & Partners in 1992. Their area of work includes projects in the field of office, shop, hotel, restaurant and apartment building.

Project Orange ist ein 1997 von James Soane und Christopher Ash gegründetes Architektur- und Designbüro in London, das aus einer 1992 lose zusammengeschlossenen Gruppe von jungen Architekten hervorging. Beide studierten Architektur in Cambridge. Ash arbeitete anschließen bei verschiedenen renommierten Büros wie Conran & Partners oder Paul Hyett, während Soane zunächst neun Jahre an der Kingston University lehrte, bevor auch er 1992 zu Conran & Partners kam. Ihr Arbeitsgebiet umfasst Projekte im Bereich Büro-, Laden-, Hotel-, Restaurant- und Wohnungsbau.

Project Orange est un bureau d'architecture et de design, fondé en 1997 à Londres par James Soane et Christopher Ash, et qui est né d'un groupe de jeunes architectes qui se sont mis en 1992 à travailler librement ensemble. Les deux architectes ont étudiés l'architecture à Cambridge. Ash a travaillé juste après dans plusieurs bureaux renommés comme Conran & Partners ou Paul Hyett, alors que Soane a tout d'abord enseigné pendant neuf ans à l'Université de Kingston, avant d'arriver lui aussi chez en 1992 chez Conran & Partners. Leur domaine de travail comprend des projets de construction de bureaux, de magasins, d'hôtels, de restaurants, et de logements.

Project Orange es una oficina de arquitectura y diseño fundada en Londres en 1997 por James Soane y Christopher Ash que resultó de un grupo formado libremente por jóvenes arquitectos. Ambos estudiaron arquitectura en Cambridge. Después de ello, Ash trabajó en diferentes oficinas de renombre como Conran & Partners o Paul Hyett mientras que Soane primero dio clases durante nueve años en la Kingston University antes de que él también entrase en Conran & Partners en 1992. Su campo de trabajo abarca proyectos en el terreno de la construcción de oficinas, tiendas, hoteles, restaurantes y viviendas.

Project Orange è uno studio di architettura e design che è stato fondato a Londra nel 1997 da James Soane e Christopher Ash a partire dall'esperienza di un gruppo di giovani architetti formatosi nel 1992. Entrambi hanno studiato architettura a Cambridge. Ash ha lavorato dopo la laurea in diversi studi rinomati quali per esempio Conran & Partners o Paul Hyett, mentre Soane si è dedicato dapprima all'esperienza didattica (per ben nove anni alla Kingston University) prima di approdare allo studio Conran & Partners nel 1992. I loro progetti spaziano dalla progettazione di uffici, negozi, hotel e ristoranti alla progettazione di spazi abitativi.

Andrée Putman

Andrée Putman, born in 1925 in Paris, began her career as a journalist in the 1960s. Various jobs for different design and marketing agencies followed. In 1978, she established the Ecart office for interior design and in 1997, her current company, Andrée Putman S.A.R.L. Her designs for museums, shops, offices, furniture or jewelry are characterized by natural elegance and an unmistakeable style. Within a few years, she was in demand as an international designer: private apartments belong to her works just as much as luxury hotels in New York and Wolfsburg, Concord's interior design or the offices of French government ministers.

Andrée Putman, 1925 in Paris geboren, begann in den 60er Jahren als Journalistin. Es folgten Stationen bei diversen Design- und Marketingagenturen. 1978 gründete sie das Büro Ecart für Interieur Design, 1997 ihr heutiges Unternehmen Andrée Putman S.A.R.L. Natürliche Eleganz und ein unverwechselbarer Stil kennzeichnen ihre Entwürfe für Museen, Geschäfte, Büroräume, Möbel oder Schmuck. Innerhalb weniger Jahre wurde sie zu einer gefragten Designerin weltweit: Privatwohnungen gehören genauso zu ihren Werken wie Luxushotels in New York und Wolfsburg, das Innendesign der Concorde oder die Büros französischer Minister.

Andrée Putman, née à Paris en 1925, a commencé à travailler comme journaliste dans les années soixante. Ont suivi ensuite plusieurs expériences dans des agences de design et de marketing. En 1978, elle a fondé le bureau de design intérieur Ecart et en 1997 l'entreprise actuelle Andrée Putman S.A.R.L. C'est une élégance naturelle et un style remarquable qui caractérisent les projets qu'elle développe pour des musées, des magasins, des bureaux, des meubles ou des bijoux. Elle est devenue en quelques années une designer internationalement demandée : on compte parmi ses œuvres aussi bien des appartements privées que des hôtels de luxe à New York et Wolfsburg, que le design intérieur du Concorde ou les bureaux ministériels français.

Andrée Putman, nacida en París en 1925, comenzó como periodista en los años 60. Siguieron estaciones en diversas agencias de diseño y marketing. En 1978 fundó la oficina de diseño interior Ecart, en 1997 su actual empresa Andrée Putman S.A.R.L.

Una elegancia natural y un estilo inconfundible caracterizan sus proyectos para museos, comercios, oficinas, muebles o joyas. En el transcurso de pocos años se convirtió en una diseñadora solicitada mundialmente: las viviendas privadas pertenecen a sus obras igual que los hoteles de lujo en Nueva York y Wolfsburg, el diseño interior del Concorde o las oficinas de ministros franceses.

Nata a Parigi nel 1925, Andrée Putman ha iniziato la sua carriera negli anni Sessanta come giornalista. Sono seguite altre tappe rappresentate dalle attività svolte in diverse agenzie di design e di marketing. Nel 1978 ha fondato lo studio d'interior design Ecart e nel 1997 la sua azienda attuale, l'Andrée Putman S.A.R.L. Eleganza naturale e stile inconfondibile caratterizzano le sue realizzazioni progettuali, che si tratti di musei, negozi e uffici o piuttosto di mobili e gioielli. Nel corso di pochi anni è diventata uno dei designer più quotati a livello internazionale. I progetti firmati Andrée Putman spaziano dalle abitazioni private ad hotel di lusso di New York e Wolfsburg, al design degli interni del Concorde fino ad arrivare agli uffici di ministri francesi.

Rockwell Group

The New York-based architecture and design firm is an amalgamation of around 150 architects, designers, artists, chefs, opera singers, dramatists and stage designers. The central concept of their work is always to blur the limits between disciplines and ideas, which initiate synergies with technology, handcraft and design. The firm has completed over 200 prize winning projects in gastronomy, education and health, theater and film. These projects include among others the Robin Hood Foundation in New York, the Motown Center in Detroit, the Kodak Theater in Hollywood and the W Hotel chain.

Die in New York ansässige Architektur- und Design-Firma ist ein Zusammenschluss von rund 150 Architekten, Designern, Künstlern, Köchen, Opernsängern, Theaterautoren und Bühnenbildnern. Kernkonzept Ihrer Arbeit ist die stete Verwischung der Grenzen zwischen den Disziplinen und Ideen, die Synergien mit Technologie, Handwerk und Design eingehen. Das Büro hat über 200, mit Preisen ausgezeichnete Projekte aus Gastronomie, Bildungs- und Gesundheitswesen, dem Theater und Film realisiert. Zu diesen Projekten

gehören u. a. die Robin Hood Stiftung New York, das Motown Center Detroit, das Kodak Theater Hollywood und die W-Hotelgruppe.

L'entreprise d'architecture et de design installée à New York est une association d'environ 150 architectes, designers, artistes, cuisiniers, chanteurs d'opéra, auteurs de théâtre et décorateurs de théâtre. Le concept fondamental de leur travail consiste à effacer constamment les frontières entre les disciplines et de développer des idées qui produisent des synergies entre technologie, artisanat et design. Le bureau a réalisé plus de 200 projets, qui ont été récompensés par des prix, dans les domaines de la restauration, de l'éducation et de la santé, du théâtre et du film. Parmi ces projets on compte entre autre celui de la Fondation Robin Hood à New York, le Centre Motown à Detroit, le Kodak Theater à Hollywood et le groupe des W hôtels.

La empresa de arquitectura y diseño establecida en Nueva York es una agrupación de alrededor de 150 arquitectos, diseñadores, artistas, cocineros, cantantes de ópera, autores de teatro y escenógrafos. El plan básico de su trabajo es la difuminación constante de las fronteras entre las disciplinas y las ideas, que contraen sinergias con la tecnología, el trabajo manual y el diseño. La oficina ha realizado más de 200 proyectos de gastronomía, educación y sanidad, teatro y cine distinguidos con premios. Entre estos proyectos se cuentan la Fundación Robin Hood en Nueva York, el Motown Center de Detroit, el Kodak Theater de Hollywood y el grupo hotelero W.

Lo studio, con sede a New York, nasce dall'unione di circa 150 architetti, designer, artisti, cuochi, cantanti lirici, autori di teatro e scenografi. La filosofia di fondo delle opere realizzate è dettata dall'approccio interdisciplinare al fine di valorizzare gli effetti sinergetici sprigionati dall'unione di tecnologia, capacità artigianali e design. Lo studio ha ottenuto diversi riconoscimenti per la realizzazione di oltre 200 progetti nel settore gastronomico, educativo e sanitario nonché teatrale e cinematografico. Fra di essi vi sono per esempio la fondazione Robin Hood New York, il Motown Center Detroit, il Kodak Theater Hollywood e la catena dei W Hotels.

Soeren Roehrs & Laura Ravel

Soeren Roehrs, born in Hamburg in 1964, graduated in music and political science from Hamburg University in 1987. Afterwards, he studied architecture in Ottawa and Berlin and graduated in 1994 at Berlin's Technical University. Along with Laura Ravel, he supports a subversive style of Berlin architecture with squatters' charm as the Tresor and Cookies projects show. Other projects in Berlin are the Schwarzenraben restaurant, Trompete and the Keller-Bar.

Soeren Roehrs, 1964 in Hamburg geboren, schloss 1987 sein Studium der Musik- und Politikwissenschaften an der Uni Hamburg ab. Anschließend absolvierte er ein Architekturstudium in Ottawa und Berlin, das er 1994 an der TU Berlin abschloss. Zusammen mit Laura Ravel steht er für eine subversive Berliner Architektur mit Hausbesetzer-Charme wie sie das Tresor und Cookies zeigen. Weitere Projekte in Berlin sind das Restaurant Schwarzenraben, Trompete und die Keller-Bar.

Soeren Roehrs, né en 1964 à Hambourg, a terminé ses études de musicologie et de sciences politiques en 1987 à l'Université de Hambourg. Il a entrepris juste après des études d'architecture à Ottawa et Berlin et a obtenu son diplôme à l'Université technique de Berlin. Avec Laura Ravel il représente une architecte berlinoise subversive qui utilise le charme des squats comme le montre des réalisations comme Tresor et Cookies. Parmi d'autres projets réalisés à Berlin, il y a le restaurant Schwarzenraben, le bar Trompete et le Keller-Bar.

Soeren Roehrs, nacido en Hamburgo en 1964, terminó su carrera de ciencias políticas y de la música en la Universidad de Hamburgo en 1987. Después de ello, estudió la carrera de arquitectura en Otawa y Berlín la cual acabó en la Universidad Técnica de Berlín en 1994. Junto con Laura Ravel es sinónimo de una arquitectura berlinesa subversiva con un encanto ocupa como lo muestran el Tresor y Cookies. Otros proyectos en Berlín son el restaurante Schwarzenrabe, Trompete y el Keller-Bar.

Soeren Roehrs, nato ad Amburgo nel 1964, si è laureato all'università di Amburgo in musicologia e scienze politiche nel 1987. In seguito ha studiato architettura ad Ottawa e Berlino, dove si è laureato nel 1994 (Univer-

sità Tecnica di Berlino). Insieme a quello di Laura Ravel, il suo nome è sinonimo di una certa tendenza architettonica sovversiva con fascino da uccupazione abusiva che va affermandosi a Berlino e che trova espressioni in locali come il Tresor e il Cookies. Ulteriori progetti realizzati a Berlino sono il ristorante Schwarzenraben, Trompete e Keller-Bar.

Rajiv Saini + Associates

The self-educated Rajiv Saini works in Mumbai as a successful architect and designer. According to Wallpaper Magazine, he now counts among the most sought after and creative up-and-coming designers. His projects, such as the Devi Garh hotel complex in Udaipur, reveal a form language which is thoroughly European, if not international. He feels obliged to his Indian roots in terms of style and experiments with modern materials, mixing them to new, fashionable styles.

Der Autodidakt Rajiv Saini ist in Mumbai als erfolgreicher Architekt und Designer tätig. Laut Wallpaper Magazine zählt er zu den derzeit begehrtesten und kreativsten unter den aufsteigenden Designern. Seine Projekte wie der Hotelkomplex Devi Garh in Udaipur zeigen eine Formensprache, die überaus europäisch, wenn nicht international ist. Im Stil fühlt er sich seinen indischen Wurzeln verpflichtet, experimentiert mit modernen Materialien und mixt diese zu neuen modischen Stilen.

Rajiv Saini est autodidacte, il est un architecte et designer à succès de Mumbai. Comme on peut le lire dans le magazine Wallpaper, il est, parmi les designers qui ont le vent en poupe, un des plus adulés et des plus créatifs du moment. Ses projets comme celui du complexe hôtelier Devi Garth à Udaipur témoignent d'un langage des formes extrêmement européen, pour ne pas dire international. Dans le style il reste fidèle à ses racines indiennes, expérimente avec des matériaux modernes et mélange les deux pour créer de nouveaux styles à la mode.

El autodidacta Rajiv Saini trabaja en Mumbai como arquitecto y diseñador de éxito. Según la revista Wallpaper, Rajiv se cuenta entre los diseñadores en auge más solicitados y creativos actualmente. Sus proyectos, como el complejo hotelero Devi Garh en Udaipur, muestran un lenguaje de formas

que es sumamente europeo si no internacional. En el estilo se siente comprometido
con sus raíces indias, experimenta con materiales modernos y los mezcla en nuevos
estilos de moda.

L'autodidatta Rajiv Saini lavora come architetto e designer di successo a Mumbai. La
rivista Wallpaper Magazine lo ha proclamato
uno dei designer più ambiti e creativi del
momento fra gli astri nascenti del design. I
suoi progetti, ad esempio il complesso alberghiero Devi Garh a Udaipur, sono espressione di un linguaggio del tutto europeo se
non addirittura internazionale. Il suo stile rivela uno stretto legame con le sue radici in-
diane nitore alla ricerca di sperimentazione
di nuovi materiali e la voglia di fondere questi elementi per coniare nuove tendenze moderne.

Schmidhuber + Partner

Schmidhuber +
Partner was found-
ed by Klaus Schmid-
huber and special-
izes in the creative
fields of land-
scape, architecture and interior. The empha-
sis is placed on the design of an unmistakable look for locations, architectures and
spatial references. Man and his individual
challenges of the design environment and
the contents and messages to be communi-
cated are at the center of considerations.
Clients include Lamborghini, Audi, Lexus,
Eon, O2 and Munich's regional central
bank.

Schmidhuber + Partner ist von Klaus
Schmidhuber gegründet worden und arbeitet im Spannungsfeld von Landschaft, Architektur und Innenraum. Der Schwerpunkt
wird dabei auf die Gestaltung eines unverwechselbaren Erscheinungsbildes von Orten,
Architekturen und räumlichen Bezügen gesetzt. Der Mensch mit seinen individuellen
Anforderungen an das gestaltete Umfeld und
die zu vermittelnden Inhalte und Botschaf-
ten steht im Zentrum der Überlegungen. Zu
den Kunden zählen Lamborghini, Audi, Lexus, Eon, O2 und die Landeszentralbank
München.

Schmidhuber + Partner a été créé par Klaus
Schmidhuber et il travaille dans le domaine

du paysage, de l'architecture et de l'espace
intérieur. Son objectif principal est de concevoir des lieux, des architectures et des rap-
ports entre les espaces que l'on reconnaît
d'emblée par leurs caractéristiques bien par-
ticulières. L'homme avec ses exigences individuelles par rapport à l'environnement créé
et les contenus et messages à transmettre
sont ici au centre des préoccupations. Parmi les clients, on compte Lamborghini, Audi, Lexus, Eon, O2 et la banque munichoise
Landeszentralbank.

Schmidhuber + Partner fue fundado por
Klaus Schmidhuber y trabaja en el campo
de tensión del paisaje, la arquitectura y los
interiores. El centro de gravedad se pone
aquí en la creación de una imagen inconfundible de lugares, arquitecturas y referencias
del espacio. El ser humano con sus requeri-
mientos individuales al entorno diseñado y
los contenidos y mensajes a transmitir está
en el centro de las reflexiones. Entre los clientes se cuentan Lamborghini, Audi, Lexus,
Eon, O2 y el banco Landeszentralbank de
Múnich.

Lo studio Schmidhuber + Partner, fondato
da Klaus Schmidhuber, è specializzato nella
progettazione paesaggistica, architettonica
e d'interni. La definizione di una fisionomia
inconfondibile di luoghi, strutture architettoniche e rapporti spaziali è il motivo di fondo
dei progetti realizzati dallo studio, che pone
al centro delle proprie riflessioni l'uomo con
le sue esigenze individuali che il contesto architettonico deve saper soddisfare nonché
contenuti e messaggi. Lamborghini, Audi,
Lexus, Eon, O2 e la Landeszentralbank München sono solo alcuni clienti dello studio
Schmidhuber + Partner.

Claudio Silvestrin Architects

Claudio Silvestrin, born in 1954, first studied
architecture in Milan with Prof. A.G. Fronzoni
and later in London. In 1989, he established
Claudio Silvestrin Architects in London. Among
his clients are names such as Giorgio Armani,
illycaffé, Calvin Klein and Cappellini. His integ-
rity, intellectual clarity, inventiveness and
love of detail are reflected in Claudio
Silvestrin's minimalist architecture: strict, but
never exaggerated, contemporary and time-
less, sober, but not ascetic, powerful without
intimidating, elegant without being pompous.

Claudio Silvestrin, geb. 1954, hat zunächst in Mailand bei Prof. A.G. Fronzoni gelernt und später in London Architektur studiert. 1989 gründete er Claudio Silvestrin Architects in London. Zu seinen Auftraggebern gehören u. a. Giorgio Armani, illycaffé, Calvin Klein und Cappellini. Seine Integrität, geistige Klarheit, sein Erfindungsgeist und die Liebe zum Detail spiegelt sich in Claudio Silvestrins minimaler Architektur: streng, aber nie übertrieben, zeitgenössisch und zeitlos, nüchtern, aber nicht asketisch, stark ohne einzuschüchtern, elegant ohne pompös zu sein.

Claudio Silvestrin, né en 1954 a tout d'abord été élève du professeur A.G. Fronzoni à Milan, et a étudié plus tard l'architecture à Londres. En 1989, il a fondé Claudio Silvestrin Architects à Londres. Parmi ses clients on trouve entre autre Giorgio Armani, illycaffé, Calvin Klein et Cappellini. Dans l'architecture minimale de Claudio Silvestrin se reflètent son intégrité, sa clarté d'esprit, son esprit inventif et son amour du détail : rigoureuse, mais sans excès, contemporaine et hors du temps, sobre mais pas ascétique, forte sans écraser, élégante sans être pompeuse.

Claudio Silvestrin, nacido en 1954, estudió arquitectura primero en Milán con el profesor A.G. Fronzoni y después en Londres. En 1989 fundó Claudio Silvestrin Architects en Londres. Entre sus clientes se cuentan, entre otros, Giorgio Armani, illycaffé, Calvin Klein y Cappellini. Su integridad, claridad intelectual, su espíritu de invención y el gusto por el detalle se reflejan en la arquitectura mínima de Claudio Silvestrin: estricta, pero nunca exagerada, contemporánea y atemporal, sobria pero no ascética, fuerte sin intimidar, elegante sin ser pomposa.

Claudio Silvestrin, nato nel 1954, si è formato dapprima a Milano alla scuola del prof. A.G. Fronzoni e poi a Londra dove ha studiato architettura. Nella capitale britannica Silvestrin ha fondato nel 1989 lo studio Claudio Silvestrin Architects. Fra i suoi clienti figurano Giorgio Armani, illycaffé, Calvin Klein e Cappellini. L'integrità, la trasparenza spirituale, lo spirito creativo e l'amore per il dettaglio si riflettono nell'architettura minimalista di Claudio Silvestrini: rigorosa ma mai in modo eccessivo, attuale ma non effimera, sobria ma non ascetica, forte nell'impatto ma non imponente, elegante senza essere pomposa.

Architekten Stadler + Partner

After studying architecture at the Technical University in Munich, Stuart Stadler established his own architectural firm in 1988. In 2000, Michael Onischke, also educated at Munich's Technical University, joined as a partner. The works of both architects are influenced by jobs with different European firms. Their main business, alongside building apartments as well as office and commercial buildings, is focused on the area of redevelopment, shop and restaurant design. Stadler's ideal of an architectural style, which creates precisely calculated moods and Onischke's experimental, lateral thinking form two sides of the same coin.

Nach dem Architekturstudium an der TU München gründete Stuart Stadler 1988 ein eigenes Architekturbüro. Im Jahre 2000 kam der ebenfalls an der Münchner TU ausgebildete Michael Onischke als Partner hinzu. Stationen bei verschiedenen europäischen Büros prägen die Arbeiten der Architekten, die neben dem Wohnungsbau sowie dem Bau von Büro- und Gewerbegebäuden ihren Tätigkeitsschwerpunkt im Bereich von Sanierungen, Laden- und Gastronomiedesign haben. Stadlers Ideal einer Baukunst, die genau kalkulierte Stimmungen kreiert, und Onischkes experimentelles Querdenken bilden gleichsam die beiden Seiten einer Medaille.

Après ses études d'architecture à l'Université Technique de Munich, Stuart Stadler a créé en 1988 son propre bureau. En l'an 2000, Michael Onischke, qui a également étudié à l'Université de Munich se joint à lui. Les expériences effectuées dans différents bureaux européens déterminent le travail des architectes qui, à côté de la construction de bâtiments d'habitations ainsi que d'immeubles commerciaux et de bureaux, ont fixé le point fort de leurs activités dans le domaine de l'assainissement et du design de magasins et de restaurants. Stadler, avec son idéal de l'art de la construction, crée des ambiances avec une précision très ajustée et Onishke poursuit ses recherches expérimentales en dehors des sentiers battus, ils forment alors les deux revers d'une même médaille.

Tras la carrera de arquitectura en la Universidad Técnica (TU) de Munich Stuart Stadler fundó en 1988 una oficina de arquitectura propia. En el año 2000 se agregó como socio Michael Onischke, también formado en la TU de Munich. Los trabajos de los arquitectos están marcados por las estaciones en diferentes oficinas europeas. Junto a la construcción de viviendas, así como la construcción de edificios de oficinas e industriales, tienen su punto central de actividad en el ámbito de los saneamientos, el diseño de tiendas y gastronomía. El ideal de Stadler de una arquitectura que crea ambientes calculados de un modo preciso y el pensamiento inconformista experimental de Onischke forman en cierto modo las dos caras de una moneda

Dopo il conseguimento della laurea presso la Università Tecnica (TU) di Monaco, Stuart Stadler ha fondato un proprio studio di architettura nel 1988. Nel 2000 vi è entrato in qualità di socio Michael Onischke, formatosi presso la stessa università. Le esperienze maturate in diversi studi di architettura europei influenzano profondamente le opere di entrambi gli architetti, che oltre ad occuparsi di edilizia residenziale, edilizia per uffici ed edilizia industriale, si sono specializzati nel campo delle ristrutturazioni, dello shop design e del dining design. L'ideale architettonico di Stadler, concepito come la concretizzazione di atmosfere accuratamente predefinite, e la sperimentazione a tutto tondo di Onischke non sono che due facce della stessa medaglia.

Philippe Starck Network

Philippe Starck, born in 1949, was educated at the Ecole de Nissim de Camondo in Paris. He is the designer of the legendary Juicy Salif lemon squeezer and probably the most individualistic and exciting designer of our time. In the 1980s, Starck developed a hotel concept for Ian Sanderson in New York that earned worldwide acclaim and is still considered today as the essence of all design hotels. In 1979, he founded the firm Starck Products and since then his unmistakable design of furniture, kitchen and bathroom accessories, as well as his highly respected interior designs, have influenced the lifestyle of many people.

Philippe Starck, 1949 geboren, erhielt seine Ausbildung an der Ecole de Nissim de Ca-

mondo in Paris. Er ist Designer der legendären Zitronenpresse Juicy Salif und der wohl eigenwilligste und aufregendste Designer unserer Zeit. In den 80er Jahren entwickelt Starck für Ian Sanderson in New York ein Hotelkonzept, das ein weltweites Echo fand und bis heute als Inbegriff aller Design-Hotels gilt. 1979 gründete er die Firma Starck Products und seither prägt er mit seinem unverwechselbaren Design von Möbeln, Küchen- und Badaccessoires sowie mit seinen viel beachteten Interieurgestaltungen den Lebensstil vieler Menschen.

Philippe Starck, né en 1949, a été formé à l'Ecole de Nissim de Camondo à Paris. C'est le designer du célèbre presse-citron Juicy Salif et il est le designer le plus original et le plus intéressant de notre temps. Dans les années quatre-vingt, Starck a développé pour Ian Sanderson à New York un concept d'hôtel qui a reçu un écho dans le monde entier et qui est aujourd'hui encore l'emblème de tous les hôtels de designers. En 1979 il a fondé la firme Starck Products et il joue depuis, avec son design de meubles, accessoires de cuisines et de salles de bains très caractéristique ainsi qu'avec ses conceptions d'espaces intérieurs, un rôle prédominant dans le style de vie de beaucoup de gens.

Philippe Starck, nacido en 1949, recibió su formación en la Ecole de Nissim de Camondo en París. Es el diseñador de la legendaria exprimidora de limones Juicy Salif y probablemente el diseñador más original y excitante de nuestro tiempo. En los años 80 Starck desarrolló un plan de hotel para Ian Sanderson en Nueva York que ha tenido un eco mundial estando considerado hasta hoy como el prototipo de todos los hoteles de diseño. En 1979 fundó la empresa Starck Products caracterizando desde entonces el estilo de vida de muchas personas con su diseño inconfundible de muebles, accesorios de cocina y baño así como con sus creaciones de interiores muy bien consideradas.

Philippe Starck, nato nel 1949, si è formato all'Ecole de Nissim de Camondo a Parigi. È l'autore del leggendario spremiagrumi Juicy Salif ed è sicuramente uno dei designer più creativi e originali della nostra epoca. Negli anni Ottanta la progettazione di un hotel per Ian Sanderson a New York, tuttora considerata espressione per eccellenza del design alberghiero, gli ha valso fama internazionale. Nel 1979 ha creato una propria azienda di produzione, la Starck Products. Da allora il suo design inconfondibile di mobili ed accessori per la cucina e il bagno nonché i suoi progetti d'interni di successo sono il sinonimo di uno stile di vita a cui si ispirano molte persone.

diseño de interiores, la configuración de fachadas, el diseño de tiendas, muebles y productos se cuentan entre los campos de trabajo de Strack. Realizó proyectos para el restaurante Die Ente von Lehel en Wiesbaden, para Toni Gard Fashion en Düsseldorf y Daniel Hechter Sport en Hannover.

Udo Strack

Udo Strack, born in 1965 in Worms, first trained as a carpenter in Hamburg. After graduating in architecture in 1995, he worked in Hamburg for Peter Schmidt Studios. In 2000, he founded the agency Udo Strack Corporate Concepts. Strack's field of work includes the design of individual brand profiles, as well as interior design, façade design, shop, furniture and product design. He completed projects for Die Ente von Lehel in Wiesbaden, Toni Gard Fashion in Düsseldorf and Daniel Hechter Sport in Hanover.

Udo Strack, 1965 in Worms geboren, absolvierte zunächst eine Ausbildung zum Tischler in Hamburg. Nach Abschluss seines Architekturstudium 1995 arbeitete er in Hamburg bei den Peter Schmidt Studios. 2000 gründete er die Agentur Udo Strack Corporate Concepts. Neben der Gestaltung individueller Markenprofile zählen Interior Design, Fassadengestaltung, Shop-, Möbel- und Produktdesign zu den Arbeitsfeldern von Strack. Er realisierte Projekte für Die Ente von Lehel in Wiesbaden, Toni Gard Fashion in Düsseldorf und Daniel Hechter Sport in Hannover.

Udo Strack, né à Worms en 1965, a tout d'abord fait une formation de menuisier. Après avoir terminé ses études d'architecture en 1995, il a travaillé à Hambourg dans les Peter Schmidt Studios. Il a créé an 2000 l'agence Udo Strack Corporate Concept. Parmi ses domaines de prédilection, à coté de la conception de profil de marque, il y a le design intérieur, la conception de façade, le design de magasins, de meubles et de produits. Il a réalisé des projets pour le restaurant Die Ente von Lehel à Wiesbaden, Toni Gard Fashion à Düsseldorf et Daniel Hechter Sport à Hanovre.

Udo Strack, nacido en Worms en 1965, se formó primero como carpintero en Hamburgo. Tras acabar su carrera de arquitectura en 1995 trabajó en Hamburgo en los Peter Schmidt Studios. En 2000 fundó la agencia Udo Strack Corporate Concepts. Junto al diseño de perfiles de marcas individuales, el

Udo Strack, nato a Worms nel 1965, ha compiuto prima un corso di formazione professionale per falegnami. Dopo aver concluso gli studi di architettura nel 1995 ha iniziato a lavorare dapprima ad Amburgo presso lo studio Peter Schmidt Studios. Nel 2000 ha fondato l'agenzia Udo Strack Corporate Concepts. Fra le attività di rilievo vanno sottolineati, oltre alla personalizzazione di alcuni brand, i lavori realizzati nei settori interior design, progettazione facciate, shop design, design di mobili e product design. Il ristorante Die Ente von Lehel, i negozi Toni Gard Fashion a Düsseldorf e Daniel Hechter Sport a Hannover sono solo alcune delle sue realizzazioni.

Studio Delrosso

Federico Delrosso, born in 1964, studied architecture in Milan and opened the Studio Delrosso in his native city of Biella. The firm's works are distinguished by the interplay of transparency, light and shadow and their focus is on the fields of architecture, interior and design. A bank in Lugano, a restaurant in Monte Carlo and ambitious apartment buildings count amongst the most recent projects. A relocation of the office to Milan is planned for spring 2005.

Federico Delrosso, 1964 geboren, studierte Architektur in Mailand und eröffnete in seiner Geburtsstadt Biella das gleichnamige Studio Delrosso. Die Arbeiten des Büros, dessen Schwerpunkt in den Bereichen Architektur, Interieur und Design liegt, zeichnen sich durch ein Zusammenspiel von Transparenz, Licht und Schatten aus. Zu den jüngsten Projekten zählen eine Bank in Lugano, ein Restaurant in Monte Carlo und ambitionierte Wohnbauten. Für das Frühjahr 2005 ist ein Umzug des Büros nach Mailand geplant.

Federico Delrosso, né en 1964, a étudié l'architecture à Milan et a ouvert dans sa ville natale Biella le Studio Delrosso, qui porte son propre nom. Les travaux du bureau, dont les activités concernent principalement les domaines de l'architecture, l'espace intérieur et le design, se distinguent par l'interaction entre transparence, lumière et ombre. Parmi les projets les plus récents, on compte une banque à Lugano, un restaurant à Monte Carlo, et des constructions d'appartements ambitieuses. Un transfert du bureau à Milan est prévu pour le printemps 2005.

Federico Delrosso, nacido en 1964, estudió arquitectura en Milán y abrió en Biella, su ciudad natal, el Studio Delrosso del mismo nombre. Los trabajos de la oficina, cuyo centro de gravedad se halla en los ámbitos de la arquitectura, los interiores y el diseño, se caracterizan por la interacción de la transparencia, las luces y sombras. Entre los proyectos más recientes se cuentan un banco en Lugano, un restaurante en Montecarlo y ambiciosos edificios de viviendas. Para la primavera de 2005 se ha planeado un traslado de la oficina a Milán.

Nato nel 1964, Federico Delrosso ha studiato architettura a Milano ed ha fondato l'omonimo studio di architettura nella sua città natale, Biella. Le realizzazioni dello studio, specializzato in progettazione architettonica, d'interni e design, sono caratterizzate da sottili giochi di luce, ombre e trasparenze. Fra gli ultimi progetti realizzati vi sono la progettazione di una banca a Lugano, un ristorante a Monte Carlo ed ulteriori ambiziosi spazi abitativi. Per i primi mesi del 2005 è previsto il trasferimento dello studio a Milano.

studio nex

In 2001, the German architect, Ellen Rapelius, and the Catalan architect, Xavier Franquesa, founded the studio nex in Barcelona. The firm specializes in design and architecture and has projects in the area of gastronomy, corporate identity and shop construction. Rapelius and Franquesa adopt themes of the Catalan city and use this to develop new, complex patterns for their work. In 2003, they were nominated for the "FAD Prizes of architecture and interior design 2003" for the restaurant LUPINO and they were chosen for the catalogue "Barcelona's Design Year 2003".

Die deutsche Architektin Ellen Rapelius und der katalanische Architekt Xavier Franquesa gründeten 2001 das studio nex in Barcelo-

na. Das auf Design und Architektur spezialisierte Büro betätigt sich im Bereich Gastronomie, Corporate Identity und Ladenbau. Rapelius und Franquesa nehmen Themen der katalanischen Stadt auf und entwickeln daraus neue komplexe Muster für ihre Arbeit. Mit dem Restaurant LUPINO wurden sie 2003 für den „FAD Prizes of architecture and interior design 2003" nominiert und den Katalog „Barcelona's Design Year 2003" ausgewählt.

L'architecte allemande Ellen Rapelius et l'architecte catalan Xavier Franquesa ont fondé en 2001 le studio nex à Barcelone. Le bureau spécialisé dans le design et l'architecture travaille dans le domaine de la restauration, de la Corporate Identity et la construction de magasins. Ellen Rapelius et Xavier Franquesa trouvent leur inspiration dans des thèmes de la ville catalan et développent ainsi de nouveau modèles complexes pour leur travail. Avec le restaurant LUPINO, ils ont été nominés en 2003 pour le prix « FAD Prizes of architecture and interior design 2003 » et choisis pour le catalogue « Barcelona's design Year 2003 ».

La arquitecta alemana Ellen Rapelius y el arquitecto catalán Xavier Franquesa fundaron en 2001 el studio nex en Barcelona. La oficina, especializada en diseño y arquitectura, se dedica al ámbito de la gastronomía, corporate identity y construcción de tiendas. Rapelius y Franquesa recogen temas de la ciudad catalana y de ellos desarrollan nuevos modelos complejos para su trabajo. Con el restaurante LUPINO fueron nominados en 2003 para los "FAD Prizes of architecture and interior design 2003" y seleccionados para el catálogo "Barcelona's Design Year 2003".

L'architetto tedesco Ellen Rapelius e l'architetto catalano Xavier Franquesa hanno fondato lo studio nex a Barcellona nel 2001. Lo studio, specializzato in design ed architettura, opera nel settore della gastronomia, di Corporate Identity e dello shop design. Rapelius e Franquesa rielaborano temi della città catalana che interpretano dando vita a nuove complesse strutture che realizzano nei loro lavori. Con il ristorante LUPINO sono stati nominati nel 2003 per il "FAD Prizes of architecture and interior design 2003" nonché scelti per il catalogo "Barcelona's Design Year 2003".

studio rcl

Richard Cutts Lundquist, born in 1958 in Washington, studied architecture in London and Berkeley. In 1990, he opened the studio rcl architectural firm, which he directs today with his partner, Sookja Lee, born in 1972 in Osaka. Both architects also teach at the Otis College of Art and Design. The ChoSun Galbee Restaurant, Best Western Inn Kelowna and apartment buildings in Santa Monica, Brentwood, Hancock Park, Los Angeles and Glendale count among the many completed projects.

Richard Cutts Lundquist, 1958 in Washington geboren, studierte in London und Berkeley Architektur. 1990 eröffnete er das Architekturbüro studio rcl, das er heute mit seiner Partnerin, der 1972 in Osaka geborenen Sookja Lee führt. Beide Architekten lehren zudem am Otis College of Art and Design. Zu den zahlreichen realisierten Projekten gehören das ChoSun Galbee Restaurant, das Best Western Inn Kelowna und Wohnungsbauten in Santa Monica, Brentwood, Hancock Park, Los Angeles and Glendale.

Richard Cutts Lundquitts, né à Washington en 1958, a étudié l'architecture à Londres et à Berkeley. Il a crée en 1990 le bureau d'architecture studio rcl qu'il dirige aujourd'hui avec sa partenaire Sookja Lee, qui est née à Osaka en 1972. Les deux architectes enseignent de surcroît au Otis College of Art and Design. Parmi les nombreux projets qu'ils ont réalisés, on compte le restaurant ChoSun Galbee, le Best Western Inn Kelowna et des bâtiments d'habitations à Santa Monica, Brentwood, Hancock, Los Angeles et Glendale.

Richard Cutts Lundquist, nacido en Washington en 1958, estudió arquitectura en Londres y Berkeley. En 1990 abrió la oficina de arquitectura studio rcl que lleva actualmente con su socia Sookja Lee, nacida en Osaka en 1972. Además, ambos arquitectos dan clases en el Otis College of Art and Design. Entre los numerosos proyectos realizados se cuentan el ChoSun Galbee Restaurant, el Best Western Inn Kelowna y edificios de viviendas en Santa Monica, Brentwood, Hancock Park, Los Angeles y Glendale.

Richard Cutts Lundquist, nato a Washington nel 1958, ha studiato architettura a Londra e a Berkeley. Nel 1990 ha creato lo studio d'architettura studio rcl che oggi dirige insieme alla sua partner, Sookja Lee, nata ad Osaka nel 1972. Entrambi gli architetti insegnano inoltre all'Otis College of Art and Design. Il ChoSun Galbee Restaurant, il Best Western Inn Kelowna e gli spazi abitativi a Santa Monica, Brentwood, Hancock Park, Los Angeles e Glendale sono solo alcuni fra i numerosi progetti realizzati.

Studiomonti s.r.l.

Claudio Monti, born in 1958 in Forlì, studied architecture in Venice. After his work for Citterio & Sottsas, in 1998, he founded the Studiomonti company. Francesco Muti joined him as a partner that year. Muti, born in 1962 in Florence, graduated in architecture in 1996 from the Technical College in Milan and worked for the Teprin studio in Ravenna. Studiomonti completes projects in the fields of gastronomy, urban planning, architecture and design for Tamoil, Motorola and Armani. In 2001, the company opened a second, larger headquarters in Milan.

Claudio Monti, 1958 in Forlì geboren, studierte Architektur in Venedig. Nach seiner Arbeit bei Citterio & Sottsas gründete er 1998 das Büro Studiomonti. Im selben Jahr kam Francesco Muti als Partner hinzu. Muti, 1962 in Florenz geboren, schloss sein Architekturstudium 1996 an der Technischen Hochschule in Mailand ab und war für das Büro Teprin in Ravenna tätig. Studiomonti realisiert Projekte aus den Bereichen Gastronomie, Städtebau, Architektur und Design für Tamoil, Motorola und Armani. 2001 eröffnete das Büro einen zweiten, größeren Hauptsitz in Mailand.

Claudio Monti, né en 1958 à Forlì, a étudié l'architecture à Venise. Après avoir travaillé chez Citterio & Sottsas il a fondé en 1998 le bureau Studio Monti. Francesco Muti s'associe au projet l'année même. Muti, né à Florence en 1962, a fait ses études d'architecture à l'Ecole Technique de Milan et a travaillé pour le bureau Teprin à Ravenne. Studiomonti réalise des projets dans les domaines de la restauration, de l'urbanisme, de l'architecture et du design pour Tamoil, Motorola et Armani. En 2001 il a ouvert un deuxième siège plus important à Milan.

Claudio Monti, nacido en Forli en 1958, estudió arquitectura en Venecia. Después de trabajar para Citterio & Sottsas fundó la oficina Studiomonti en 1998. En el mismo año se agregó como socio Francesco Muti. Muti, nacido en Florencia en 1962, realizó su carrera de arquitectura en la Universidad Técnica de Milán y trabajó para la oficina Teprin en Rávena. Studiomonti realiza proyectos en los terrenos de la gastronomía, el urbanismo, la arquitectura y el diseño para Tamoil, Motorola y Armani. En 2001 la oficina abrió una segunda sede principal más grande en Milán.

Nato a Forlì nel 1958, Claudio Monti ha studiato architettura a Venezia. Dopo l'esperienza lavorativa presso lo studio Citterio & Sottsas, ha fondato lo studio Studiomonti 1998. Nello stesso anno Francesco Muti è diventato socio dello studio. Muti, nato a Firenze nel 1962, si è laureato in architettura al Politecnico di Milano nel 1996 ed ha lavorato per lo studio Teprin di Ravenna. Studiomonti ha realizzato progetti nel settore gastronomico, urbanistico, architettonico e design per Tamoil, Motorola e Armani. Nel 2001 Studiomonti ha aperto un secondo studio più ampio con sede a Milano.

Suppose Design Office

Makoto Tanijiri, born in 1974 in Hiroshima, opened the suppose design office in 2000. He previously worked from 1994 to 1999 for Motokane Architect and from 1999 to 2000 for HAL Architects. The small, currently three-man creative team has recently completed several buildings in Ushita, Misonou, Bishamon and Oto-ya. The works of suppose design have already been awarded several prizes, among others, the "Urban Design Award Hiroshima" and the "JCD Design Award".

Makoto Tanijiri, 1974 in Hiroshima geboren, eröffnete im Jahr 2000 das suppose design office. Zuvor arbeitete er von 1994 bis 1999 bei Motokane Architect und von 1999 bis 2000 bei HAL Architects. Das kleine, derzeit dreiköpfige kreative Büro hat aktuell mehrere Bauten in Ushita, Misonou, Bishamon und Oto-ya fertig gestellt. Die Arbeiten von suppose design sind bereits mit verschiedenen Preisen ausgezeichnet worden, u. a. mit dem „Urban Design Award Hiroshima" und dem „JCD Design Award".

Makoto Tanijiri, né à Hiroshima en 1974, a créé le suppose design office en l'an 2000. Il a travaillé auparavant de 1994 à 1999 chez Motokane Architect et de 1999 à 2000 chez HAL Architects. Le petit bureau très créatif, qui est composé actuellement de trois personnes, a déjà réalisé pour l'instant plusieurs constructions à Ushita, Misonou, Bishamon et Oto-ya. Les travaux de suppose design office ont déjà reçu plusieurs prix, parmi lesquels celui du « Urban Design Award Hiroshima » et celui du « JCD Design Award ».

Makoto Tanijiri, nacido en Hiroshima en 1974, abrió la suppose design office en el año 2000. Antes de ello había trabajado de 1994 a 1999 para Motokane Architect y de 1999 a 2000 para HAL Architects. La pequeña oficina creadora, actualmente de tres personas, ha terminado en la actualidad varios edificios en Ushita, Misonou, Bishamon y Oto-ya. Los trabajos de suppose design ya han sido distinguidos con varios premios, entre otros, con el "Urban Design Award Hiroshima" y el "JCD Design Award".

Nato a Hiroshima nel 1974, Makoto Tanijiri ha fondato lo studio suppose design office nel 2000, dopo aver lavorato dal 1994 al 1999 presso lo studio Motokane Architect e dal 1999 al 2000 presso lo studio HAL Architects. Questo piccolo e creativo studio, che attualmente consta di tre collaboratori, ha realizzato di recente progetti a Ushita, Misonou, Bishamon e Oto-ya. Le opere di suppose design hanno già vinto diversi premi, fra cui i riconoscimenti "Urban Design Award Hiroshima" e "JCD Design Award".

Tag Front

After a stay in Europe, the Lebanese brothers Mehdi Rafaty, born in 1968, and Mandi Rafaty, born in 1964, relocated in 1997 to Los Angeles, where they founded Tag Front in 1998. They both completed their architectural studies at the Southern California Institute of Architecture. Tag Front describes its design style as "Cuban modernist", a mix of Spanish elements with Lebanese influence, combined with original details. Their works have not only been awarded classical architectural prizes, but the firm was also honored as one of the leading design agencies in Los Angeles.

Die libanesischen Brüder Mehdi Rafaty, geb. 1968, und Mandi Rafaty, geb. 1964, sind nach einem Aufenthalt in Europa 1997 nach Los Angeles übergesiedelt, wo sie Tag Front 1998 gegründet haben. Gemeinsam schlossen sie ihr Architekturstudium am Southern California Institute of Architecture ab. Tag Front bezeichnet seinen Designstil als „Cuban modernist", einem Mix aus spanischen Elementen mit libanesischem Einfluss, kombiniert mit ausgearbeiteten Details. Ihre Arbeiten haben nicht nur klassische Architekturpreise erhalten, sondern das Büro wurde auch als eine der führenden Designagenturen in Los Angeles geehrt.

Les frères libanais Mehdi Rafaty, né en 1968 et Mandi Rafaty, né en 1964, ont après un séjour en Europe en 1997, émigré vers Los Angeles où ils ont créé Tag Front. Ils ont étudié ensemble l'architecture au Southern California Institute of Architecture. Tag Front décrit son style de design comme « cuban modernist », un mélange d'éléments espagnols et d'influence libanaise, associés à des détails soignés. Leurs travaux ont non seulement reçu des prix d'architecture classiques, mais leur bureau a aussi eu l'honneur d'être désigné comme l'une des agences de design les plus importantes de Los Angeles.

Los hermanos libaneses Mehdi Rafaty, nacido en 1968, y Mandi Rafaty, nacido en 1964, se trasladaron a Los Angeles en 1997 tras una estancia en Europa fundando allí Tag Front en 1998. Juntos estudiaron arquitectura en el Southern California Institute of Architecture. Tag Front describe su estilo de diseño "Cuban modernist", una mezcla de elementos hispanos con influencia libanesa combinada con los detalles elaborados. Sus trabajos no han recibido solamente premios clásicos de arquitectura sino que la oficina también fue honrada como una de las agencias de diseño más importantes de Los Angeles.

Dopo un soggiorno in Europa i due fratelli libanesi Mehdi Rafaty, nato nel 1968, e Mandi Rafaty, nato nel 1964, si sono trasferiti a Los Angeles nel 1997 dove, nel 1998, hanno fondato Tag Front. Entrambi studiato architettura presso l'università Southern California Institute of Architecture. Tag Front definisce il suo stile di design come "Cuban modernist", una combinazione di elementi spagnoli ed influssi libanesi arricchiti da dettagli elaborati. Fra i riconoscimenti ottenuti

figurano non solo premi classici di architettura bensì anche il riconoscimento come una delle agenzie di spicco nel settore del design a Los Angeles.

Ascan Tesdorpf

Ascan Tesdorpf, born in Mannheim in 1962, studied architecture in Stuttgart and London from 1984–1991. Afterwards, he worked for architectural studios in London, Stuttgart and Berlin, where he opened his own office in 1997. Tesdorpf builds rooms to relax in. His use of architectural methods for this purpose is economic, concentrated and precisely tailored to the job. He reduces material, structure and construction to such an extent that these blend into the background and create a feel-good atmosphere. He is a master of the art of creating "incidental" rooms, which are nevertheless unmistakable and also possess a latent and lasting power of identification.

Ascan Tesdorpf, 1962 in Mannheim geboren, studierte 1984–1991 Architektur in Stuttgart und London. Danach arbeitete er für Architekturbüros in London, Stuttgart und Berlin, wo er 1997 ein eigenes Büro eröffnete. Tesdorpf baut Räume zum Wohlfühlen. Dazu nutzt er architektonische Mittel knapp, konzentriert und präzise auf den Bedarf abgestimmt. Material, Struktur und Konstruktion reduziert er soweit, dass diese zurücktreten und eine stimmige Atmosphäre schaffen. Er beherrscht die Kunst „beiläufige" Räume zu schaffen, die dennoch unverwechselbar sind und eine ebenso unterschwellige wie nachhaltige Identifikationskraft besitzen.

Ascan Esdorf, né en 1962 à Mannheim, a étudié de 1984 à 1991 l'architecture à Stuttgart et à Londres. Il a travaillé ensuite dans des bureaux d'architecture à Londres, Stuttgart et Berlin, où il a ouvert son propre bureau en 1997. Tesdorf crée des espaces pour qu'on s'y sente bien. Pour cela, il utilise sans excès des moyens architectoniques qui sont adaptés au besoin d'une façon concentrée et précise. Il réduit les matériaux, la structure et la construction à leur simple fonction, de manière à ce qu'ils passent au second plan et créent ainsi une atmosphère cohérente. Il a un vrai talent pour créer des espaces « qui n'ont l'air de rien » mais qui pourtant ont un caractère unique et possèdent un pouvoir d'identification à la fois sous-jacent et durable.

Ascan Tesdorpf, nacido en 1962 en Mannheim, estudió arquitectura en Stuttgart y Londres entre 1984 y 1991. Después trabajó para oficinas de arquitectura en Londres, Stuttgart y Berlín donde abrió una oficina propia en 1997. Tesdorpf construye espacios para sentirse bien. Para ello aprovecha los medios arquitectónicos de manera concisa, concentrada y precisa, ajustados a las necesidades. Reduce el material, la estructura y la construcción por lo que éstos pasan a un segundo plano creando una atmósfera armónica. Domina el arte de crear espacios "casuales" que, no obstante, son inconfundibles y poseen un poder de identificación tanto subliminal como duradero.

Nato a Mannheim nel 1962, Ascan Tesdorpf ha studiato architettura a Stoccarda e Londra fra il 1984 e il 1991. In seguito ha maturato rilevanti esperienze presso studi di architettura a Londra, Stoccarda e Berlino prima di fondare un proprio studio nella capitale tedesca nel 1997. Gli spazi creati da Tesdorpf sono ambienti che trasmettono una sensazione de benessere. Li caratterizza l'uso moderato dei mezzi espressivi che Tesdorpf dosa con parsimonia correlandoli rigorosamente alle esigenze. Materiali, struttura ed elementi architettonici vengono minimizzati fino quasi a scomparire per esaltare, unica protagonista, un'atmosfera armoniosa. È maestro nell'arte dell'inscenare con "nonchalance", dando vita ad una contraddizione solo apparente con lo stile inconfondibile e la forte suggestività, impercettibile e tutt'altro che effimera, che contraddistingono gli spazi da lui firmati.

Frank B. Theuerkauf

Frank Theuerkauf lives in Bardowick and his firm Wohnphilosophie Frank Theuerkauf Konception und Design focuses above all on the field of industrial design, consulting and interior architecture. Theuerkauf has a mutli-faceted repertoire due to experimenting with and mixing materials and he uses this in the most diverse interior design plans. This approach also influenced the mix of old and new, of inner and outer space in the high profile re-development of the Turnhalle St. Georg near Hamburg.

Der in Hamburg lebende Frank Theuerkauf ist mit seinem Büro Wohnphilosophie Frank Theuerkauf Konzeption und Design vor allem im Bereich Industriedesign, Beratung und Innenarchitektur tätig. Durch Experimentieren und Mixen von Materialien verfügt Theuerkauf über ein vielseitiges Repertoire, das er in verschiedenste Interieurkonzepte einbringt. Dies prägte auch den Mix aus Alt und Neu, zwischen Innen- und Außenraum beim viel beachteten Umbau der Turnhalle St. Georg bei Hamburg.

Frank Theuerkauf vit à Bardowick et travaille avec son bureau Wohnphilosophie Frank Theuerkauf Konzeption und Design principalement dans les domaines du design industriel, du conseil et de l'architecture d'intérieur. En expérimentant et en mélangeant les matériaux, Frank Theuerkauf s'est constitué un large répertoire qu'il utilise pour créer ses concepts d'intérieur les plus variés. Cela caractérise aussi la conjugaison de l'ancien et du neuf, des espaces intérieurs et extérieurs qu'il a mise en œuvre lors de la rénovation très remarquée du Turnhalle St. Georg à Hambourg.

Frank Theuerkauf, que vive en Bardowick, trabaja con su oficina Wohnphilosophie Frank Theuerkauf Konzeption und Design sobre todo en el ámbito del diseño industrial, la asesoría y la arquitectura de interiores. Por medio de la experimentación y la mezcla de materiales Theuerkauf dispone de un repertorio variado que lleva a los proyectos de interiores más diferentes. Esto marcó también la mezcla de lo viejo y lo nuevo, entre el espacio interior y el exterior en la reforma –muy bien considerada– del Turnhalle St. Georg Hamburgo.

Lo studio Wohnphilosophie Frank Theuerkauf Konzeption und Design, fondato dall'omonimo designer residente ad Bardowick, opera nel settore dell'industrial design, della consulenza e dell'architettura d'interni. La sperimentazione e la combinazione insolita di materiali gli ha permesso di crearsi un policromatico repertorio da cui affiorano le concezioni più svariate di interior design. È questo il principio ispiratore che ha guidato la combinazione di vecchio e nuovo nonché l'integrazione fra spazio interno ed esterno nella apprezzata ristrutturazione della Turnhalle St. Georg a Amburgo.

Tihany Design

Adam D. Tihany was born in 1948 in Siebenbürgen and grew up in Israel. He studied architecture in Milan, then he worked for European design firms and moved to New York in 1976, where he founded a design studio in 1978. Tihany created several of the world's leading restaurants and hotels and successfully works in the area of product design. In 2004, Adam D. Tihany was awarded the "Prix Villégiature" for the design of the Aleph Hotel in Rome. Since 1991, he has had a place in the Interior Design Hall of Fame. Tihany is an honorary doctor of the New York School of Interior Design.

Adam D. Tihany wurde 1948 in Siebenbürgen geboren und wuchs in Israel auf. Er studierte Architektur in Mailand, arbeitete anschließend bei europäischen Designbüros und zog 1976 nach New York, wo er 1978 ein Designstudio gründete. Tihany kreierte einige der weltweit herausragendsten Restaurants und Hotels und ist erfolgreich im Bereich des Produktdesigns tätig. Adam D. Tihany empfing 2004 den „Prix Villégiature" für die Gestaltung des Aleph Hotels in Rom. Seit 1991 hat er einen Platz in der Interior Design Hall of Fame. Tihany ist Ehrendoktor der New York School of Interior Design.

Adam D. Tihany est né en 1948 à Siebenbürgen et a grandi en Israël. Il a fait ses études d'architecture à Milan, à la suite desquelles il a travaillé dans des bureaux de design européens et il est parti à New York en 1976 où il a fondé en 1978 un studio de design. Tihany a créé quelques-uns des restaurants et hôtels les plus remarquables du monde et travaille avec beaucoup de succès dans le domaine du design industriel. Adam D. Tihany a reçu en 2004 le « Prix Villégiature » pour la conception de l'hôtel Aleph à Rome. Depuis 1991, il a une place à l'Interior Design Hall of Fame. Tihany est docteur honoris causa à la School of Interior Design de New York.

Adam D. Tihany nació en Siebenbürgen en 1948 y creció en Israel. Estudió arquitectura en Milán, a continuación trabajó en oficinas de diseño europeas y en 1976 se trasladó a Nueva York donde fundó un estudio de diseño en 1978. Tihany creó algunos de los restaurantes y hoteles más destacados mundialmente y trabaja con éxito en el ámbito del diseño de productos. Adam D. Tihany recibió en 2004 el "Prix Villégiature" por el diseño del Aleph Hotel en Roma. Desde 1991 tiene un lugar en el Interior Design Hall of Fame. Tihany es doctor honoris causa de la New York School of Interior Design.

Nato a Siebenbürgen nel 1948, Adam D. Tihany è cresciuto in Israele. Dopo aver studiato architettura a Milano, inizia a lavorare presso studi di design europei prima di trasferirsi a New York nel 1976 dove, nel 1978, fonda un suo studio di design. Tihany ha creato alcuni dei ristoranti e degli hotel di maggior rilievo internazionale ed opera con successo nel campo del product design. Nel 2004 Adam D. Tihany ha vinto il premio "Prix Villégiature" per il miglior interior design in Europa realizzato per l'Aleph Hotel di Roma. Dal 1991 è entrato a far parte dell'olimpo del prestigioso Interior Design Hall of Fame. Tihany è stato inoltre insignito del titolo di dottore ad honorem dalla New York School of Interior Design.

Johannes Torpe Studios

Johannes Torpe was born in Copenhagen in 1973. At an early age, he gained experience as a musician and lighting designer. At the age of seventeen, with his background, he started a firm for lighting design that quickly made him the most famous lighting designer in Denmark. After studying graphic design as well, he changed to interior design and he also works in the field of product design. The Johannes Torpe Studios count among Denmark's most important firms with their innovative projects. Since 2002, his brother, Rune Reilly Küisch, who work as a DJ, has contributed music as the creative part.

Johannes Torpe wurde 1973 in Kopenhagen geboren. Schon früh sammelte er Erfahrung als Musiker und Lichtdesigner. Mit diesem Hintergrund eröffnete er im Alter von 17 Jahren eine Firma für Lichtdesign, mit der er schnell zum berühmtesten Lichtdesigner Dänemarks wurde. Nach einem zusätzlichen Studium des Grafikdesign wechselte er zum Interior Design und ist zudem in Bereichen des Produktdesigns tätig. Die Johannes Torpe Studios zählen mit ihren innovativen Projekten zu den bedeutendsten Büros Dänemarks. Seit 2002 bringt sein Bruder Rune Reilly Küisch als DJ die Musik als kreativen Part ein.

Johannes Torpe est né à Copenhague en 1973. Il a acquis très tôt une expérience en tant que musicien et designer lumière. C'est dans ce contexte qu'il a ouvert à l'âge de 12 ans une firme de design de lumière avec laquelle il est devenu très vite le designer lumière le plus célèbre du Danemark. Après des études supplémentaires de graphisme, il devient designer d'intérieur et travaille de surcroît dans le domaine du design de produits. Les Studios Johannes Torpe avec leurs projets innovants comptent parmi les plus importants du Danemark. Depuis 2002 son frère Rune Reilly Küisch a introduit, en tant que DJ, la musique comme élément de création.

Johannes Torpe nació en Copenhage en 1973. Pronto reunió experiencia como músico y diseñador de iluminación. Con este trasfondo abrió una empresa de diseño de iluminación a la edad de 17 años con la que se convirtió rápidamente en el diseñador de iluminación más famoso de Dinamarca. Tras una carrera adicional de diseño gráfico se pasó al diseño de interiores y, además, trabaja en el terreno del diseño de productos. Con sus proyectos innovadores los Johannes Torpe Studios se cuentan entre las oficinas más importantes de Dinamarca. Desde 2002 su hermano Rune Reilly Küisch, como discjockey, aporta la música como la parte creativa.

Johannes Torpe è nato a Kopenhagen nel 1973. Formatosi all'esperienza precoce maturata come musicista e lighting designer, Torpe crea all'età di 17 anni una ditta di lighting design con la quale si afferma velocemente fino a diventare il lighting designer più rinomato di tutta la Danimarca. Dopo essersi cimentato con gli studi di graphic design, Torpe si dedica all'interior design facendo svariate esperienze nel campo del product design. Con i loro innovativi progetti, gli Johannes Torpe Studios sono fra gli studi più gettonati di tutta la Danimarca. Dal 2002 Rune Reilly Küisch, arricchisce, con la sua attività di DJ, l'impatto dei lavori del fratello designer conferendo loro un'ulteriore dimensione musicale.

Architekturbüro Franziska Ullmann und Peter Ebner

Franziska Ullmann graduated from architectural studies at the Technical University of Vienna. She teaches in the Prof. Hollein master class at the College for Applied Art in Vienna and since 1995, she has been a professor at Stuttgart University. In 1998, she founded a joint studio with Peter Ebner in Vienna. Ebner studied architecture in Graz and Los Angeles and in his peer group he counted among those who went their own way and ignored fashionable trends. He is the Chairman of the Architekture Initiative in Salzburg and in his spare time he works as a guest critic for the Harvard Graduate School of Design in Boston.

Franziska Ullmann absolvierte ihr Architekturstudium an der TU Wien. Sie hat eine Lehrtätigkeit an der Hochschule für angewandte Kunst Wien, Meisterklasse Prof. Hollein, und ist seit 1995 Professor an der Universität Stuttgart. 1998 gründete sie mit Peter Ebner in Wien ein gemeinsames Büro. In seiner Generation zählt Ebner, der in Graz und Los Angeles Architektur studierte, zu jenen, die abseits der modischen Tendenzen individuelle Wege gehen. Er ist Vorsitzender der Initiative Architektur in Salzburg und nebenbei Gastkritiker an der Harvard Graduate School of Design in Boston.

Franziska Ullmann a obtenu son diplôme d'architecture à l'Université Technique de Vienne. Elle enseigne à l'Ecole Supérieure d'Arts Appliqués de Vienne, dans la classe dirigée par le Professeur Hollein et est depuis 1995 professeur à l'Université de Stuttgart. Elle a fondé en 1998 avec Peter Ebner un bureau à Vienne. Peter Ebner, qui a étudié l'architecture à Graz et Los Angeles, compte dans sa génération parmi ceux qui suivent leurs propres voies en dehors des tendances à la mode. Il est président de Initiative Architektur à Salzbourg et aussi critique invité à la Harvard Graduate School of Design de Boston.

Franziska Ullmann realizó su carrera de arquitectura en la Universidad Técnica de Viena. Da clases en la Universidad de artes aplicadas de Viena –en la clase magistral del profesor Hollein– y desde 1995 es profesora en la Universidad de Stuttgart. En 1998 fundó con Peter Ebner una oficina conjunta en Viena. Dentro de su generación Ebner, que estudió arquitectura en Graz y Los Angeles, se cuenta entre los que siguen caminos individuales fuera de las tendencias de moda. Es presidente de Initiative Architektur en Salzburgo y, junto a ello, crítico invitado en la Harvard Graduate School of Design en Boston.

Franziska Ullmann ha compiuto i suoi studi di architettura all'Università Tecnica (TU) di Vienna. Svolge un'attività didattica all'Accademia delle Arti Applicative di Vienna, Meisterklasse Prof. Hollein, e dal 1995 è titolare di cattedra all'università di Stoccarda. Nel 1998 ha fondato uno studio d'architettura a Vienna insieme a Peter Ebner. Ebner, che ha studiato architettura a Graz e Los Angeles, è fra gli esponenti della sua generazione che alle mode effimere hanno preferito un percorso tutto individuale. È presidente dell'Initiative Architektur Salzburg e visiting critic alla Harvard Graduate School of Design di Boston.

unit-berlin

unit-berlin, is Berlin's new design firm of Heike Dertmann, Hinnerk Dedecke and Thilo Fuchs. Following several projects in the fields of trade fair and exhibition architecture, as well as the award-winning works in communication design, "red dot, best of the best 2003", an innovative brand architecture was thought up and completed for Tressette, as part of a comprehensive, international corporate design.

unit-berlin, ist das junge Berliner Gestaltungsbüro von Heike Dertmann, Hinnerk Dedecke und Thilo Fuchs. Nach mehreren Projekten in den Bereichen Messe- und Ausstellungsarchitektur sowie mit dem „red dot, best of the best 2003" preisgekrönten Arbeiten im Kommunikationsdesign wurde für Tressette eine innovative Markenarchitektur als Teil eines umfassenden internationalen Corporate Design konzipiert und realisiert.

unit-berlin est le bureau de conception berlinois de Heike Dertmann, Hinnerk Debecke et Thilo Fuchs. Après plusieurs projets dans le domaine de l'architecture de bâtiments d'expositions et ses travaux en design de communication qui ont reçu le prix « red dot, best of the best 2003 », le bureau a conçu et réalisé pour Tresette une architecture de marque innovatrice faisant partie d'un Corporate Design qui est d'envergure internationale.

unit-berlin es la joven oficina berlinesa de diseño de Heike Dertmann, Hinnerk Dedecke y Thilo Fuchs. Después de varios proyectos en los terrenos de la arquitectura de ferias y exposiciones así como con los trabajos premiados con el "red dot, best of the best 2003" en diseño de comunicación se planeó y realizó para Tressette una arquitectura de marcas innovadora como una parte del amplio Corporate Design internacional.

unit-berlin è un giovane studio di design di Berlino di cui sono titolari Heike Dertmann, Hinnerk Dedecke e Thilo Fuchs. Fra le attività di maggior rilievo spiccano progettazione fieristica, exhibition design, attività di concept nel campo della comunicazione e dei media (per la quale lo studio è stato insignito del premio "red dot, best of the best 2003") nonché concept e realizzazione di brand design innovativo su incarico di Tressette come parte di un più ampio progetto internazionale di Corporate Design.

Other Designpocket titles by teNeues:

African Interior Design 3-8238-4563-2
Asian Interior Design 3-8238-4527-6
Avant-Garde Page Design 3-8238-4554-3
Bathroom Design 3-8238-4523-3
Beach Hotels 3-8238-4566-7
Berlin Apartments 3-8238-5596-4
Car Design 3-8238-4561-6
Cool Hotels 3-8238-5556-5
Cool Hotels America 3-8238-4565-9
Cool Hotels Asia/Pacific 3-8238-4581-0
Cool Hotels Europe 3-8238-4582-9
Cosmopolitan Hotels 3-8238-4546-2
Country Hotels 3-8238-5574-3
Exhibition Design 3-8238-5548-4
Furniture Design 3-8238-5575-1
Garden Design 3-8238-4524-1
Italian Interior Design 3-8238-5495-X
Kitchen Design 3-8238-4522-5
London Apartments 3-8238-5558-1
Los Angeles Houses 3-8238-5594-8
Miami Houses 3-8238-4545-4
New York Apartments 3-8238-5557-3
Office Design 3-8238-5578-6
Paris Apartments 3-8238-5571-9
Pool Design 3-8238-4531-4
Product Design 3-8238-5597-2
Rome Houses 3-8238-4564-0
San Francisco Houses 3-8238-4526-8
Showrooms 3-8238-5496-8
Ski Hotels 3-8238-4543-8
Spa & Wellness Hotels 3-8238-5595-6
Sport Design 3-8238-4562-4
Staircases 3-8238-5572-7
Sydney Houses 3-8238-4525-X
Tokyo Houses 3-8238-5573-5
Tropical Houses 3-8238-4544-6

Each volume:

12.5 x 18.5 cm
400 pages
c. 400 color illustrations